THE KETO COOKBOOK FOR BEGINNERS

(1500 Days of Easy-to-Make & Delicious Recipes Made with Low-Carb and Nutrient-Filled Ingredients to Maximize Weight Loss on A Budget | 28-Day Meal Plan Included)

By

Melissa Morales

Table of Contents:

TABLE OF CONTENTS

INTRODUCTION

After years of being restricted to clinical nutrition in hospitals, the ketogenic diet, sometimes referred to as the "keto diet," is making a comeback as one of the most popular diet fads in the world. The diet was created in the 1920s to treat juvenile epilepsy, and because to its extraordinary efficacy (those on the diet saw 30%–40% fewer seizures), it continues to be utilized in that field today. The phrase ketogenic diet originates in the 1930s. Yet, the diet, which relies on consuming ketones, has only recently been widely known and used as a strategy for both decreasing weight and treating diet-related illnesses like diabetes mellitus. This diet has also been demonstrated to be effective in treating depression, Alzheimer's disease, and therapy-resistant epilepsy; however, the exact causes are still unclear. Many of the people's perceptions of a healthy, nutritious diet, which normally encourages the intake of protein, fat, and carbs, are undoubtedly at odds with this eating strategy. From an evolutionary standpoint, ketosis is a typical adaptive reaction that helped people survive historical famines. Currently, a variety of low-carb diet plans have taken use of this physiological process. Such a diet involves swapping out carbohydrates for meals high in fat & protein, which, if followed for a prolonged length of time, may have negative effects on certain people. Consuming high-fat meals will likely increase your consumption of saturated fat, which is now recommended to be limited to 30 grams for men & 20 grams for women according to UK government recommendations. If you have got a renal ailment, it is assumed that eating a lot of protein would be problematic. Nonetheless, the majority of ketogenic diets provide moderate doses of protein rather than high ones.

In many ways, the ketogenic diet and the Paleo diet are identical. The latter is focused on foods that were supposedly consumed during the Paleolithic Era (Old Stone Age) before agriculture was developed: meat, fruits, fish, vegetables, and nuts, but not dairy products or grains. This diet is justified by the claim that since the human body evolved slowly, it responds better to this "natural" diet than it does to the "artificial" one that resulted from the civilization of plants & animals. The majority of a normal ketogenic diet (70–80%) is made up of fat in the form of fish, meat, lard, nuts, butter, and seeds. Proteins make up the remaining portion, with very little room left over for carbs. The so-called keto diet is not standardized in any way, with the exception of the fact that meals high in carbohydrates like pasta, bread, as well as potatoes are not permitted.

CHAPTER 1:
Keto Diet - An Introduction

The Ketogenic diet is a way of eating that emphasizes fats, moderate amounts of protein, and little carbohydrates (usually below 50g per day). It's simple enough to pick a keto diet and also be a vegetarian or vegan, so this doesn't have to include consuming fatty cheese or bacon all day. Typically, when carbohydrates are broken down, glucose is released into circulation, where it may be utilized as fuel or it can be stored as glycogen in the liver. This glycogen is freed to be utilized for energy after some weeks of a low-carb diet. If this energy reserve is exhausted, the body will start to turn to stored fat for energy. Stolen fat cells are carried to the liver, where they are transformed into ketones, which are then utilized as fuel.

- **1.1 Ketogenic Diet**

The ketogenic diet became well-liked as an epilepsy therapy in the 1920s & 1930s. It was developed to replace unorthodox fasting, which had been successful in treating epilepsy. Yet as better anticonvulsant medications became available, most people stopped following the diet. While it revealed that most instances of epilepsy could be adequately treated with these drugs, they nevertheless failed to establish epileptic control in roughly 20%-30% of epileptics.

The diet was reintroduced for these people, and especially for children with epilepsy, as a method of treating the ailment.

Almost 80% of the daily calories should come from fat, fewer than 5% should come from carbs, and 15% to 20% should come from protein on the ketogenic diet. This is quite a deviation from the typical recommendations for the proportions of protein, carbs, and fat, which are respectively 20% to 35%, 45% to 65%, and 10% to 35%. The traditional or classical keto has precise macros ratios of 4:1 or 4 parts fat (80%) to one part each carbohydrate & protein (20%). It is used for medicinal reasons. A modified keto diet, as mentioned in this article, is more often used for those who are not utilizing it for therapeutic purposes and offers a more changeable range of macros ratios: fat 65-80%, carbohydrates 5-10%, and protein 15-30%, although generally, carbs are lowered to about 50 grams. To enter the state of nutritional ketosis, you must follow a ketogenic diet. The key element of the ketogenic diet is a metabolic state known as ketosis. Typically, glucose fuels the body fairly efficiently. As the body breaks the carbs down, glucose is created. The body prefers to manufacture energy this way since it is a fairly easy procedure. Your body searches for other sources of energy to make up the difference when you reduce your carbohydrate intake and have not yet eaten in a while. Usually, the source is fat. Fat is generated from your cells & floods the liver when the blood sugar lowers as a result of not consuming enough carbohydrates. Your body utilizes ketone bodies as a backup source of energy after converting fat in ketone bodies in the liver. You enter nutritional ketosis as a consequence of an increase in ketone body levels in your blood.

- **1.2 Ketogenic Foods**

Even if you are aware that you must follow a diet that is very low in carbohydrates, rich in fat, and moderate in protein, it might be difficult to know which items to consume. Below is the list of all keto-friendly, low-carb items you can consume while adhering to the keto diet.

Seafood and fish

Low-carb vegetables

Cheese

Poultry

Eggs

Avocados

Seeds, nuts, & essential oils

Greek yogurt & cottage cheese are simple.

Berries

unsweetened tea and coffee

Dark chocolate & cocoa powder

Items You Should Avoid:

Due to the ketogenic diet's low carb consumption, it may be necessary to avoid a number of foods with higher carb counts, such as:

Grains

Fruits and vegetables with a lot of sugar

Juices

Sweetened yogurt

Any type of sugar, honey, or syrup

Crackers and chips

Baked foods, even those without gluten.

Don't get too down on yourself. There are no items that are off limits while following the keto, claim Stone and Laura Dority, RDN & LDN dietitians of the Keto Diet's Hope Foundation. It is related to your total calorie intake & how you opt to "spend" your carbs. You should generally keep your daily carbohydrate consumption between 20 and 40 grams. "However, a carb dosage may vary from 10 to 60 grams per day depending on the individual in order to initiate ketosis. Net carbs, or total sugars minus fiber, are represented by this number "says Stone.

- **1.3 Types of Keto Diets**

A keto is one that is intended to induce ketosis, which causes body fat to break down into ketones, and to enable the body to operate mostly on ketones instead of glucose. There are several techniques to induce ketosis, and thus, there are numerous variations of the ketogenic diet. While the ultimate objective of these regimens is the same, the many varieties of ketogenic diet frequently have a lot of commonalities, notably in being reduced in carbohydrates & high in dietary fat.

The SKD (Standard Ketogenic Diet):

It is a high-fat, moderate-protein, and very low-carb diet. It normally has a 70–75% fat content, 20% protein content, and 5–10% carbohydrate content. A typical normal ketogenic diet will be: in grams per day.

20–50 grams of carbohydrates

40 to 60 g of protein.

There is no established limit for fat

For a diet to be considered a ketogenic diet, fat in diet should make up the bulk of the calories. There is no cap since everyone's needs for energy might differ greatly. Vegetables should play a significant role in ketogenic diets, especially non-starchy vegetables since they have a very low carbohydrate content. Conventional ketogenic diets have repeatedly shown their ability to help patients lose weight, manage their blood sugar levels, and enhance their cardiovascular health.

Very less carb keto diet (VLCKD):

A VLCKD often refers to a normal ketogenic diet since it is extremely low in carbohydrates.

Well-Formulated Keto Diet (WFKD):

The phrase 'Well Designed Ketogenic Diet' originates from Steve Phinney, 1 of the foremost researchers on ketogenic diets. The WFKD adheres to a similar structure to the conventional ketogenic diet. When the ratios of the macronutrients fat, protein, and carbohydrate are met, the diet is said to be well-formulated, which increases the likelihood that ketosis will occur.

MCT Keto Diet:

This adheres to the general principles of the ketogenic diet but focuses on employing MCTs (medium chain triglycerides) to provide the major part of the diet's fat. Coconut oil contains MCTs, which are also present in MCT oil & MCT emulsion drinks. Due to the idea that MCTs enable patients to eat more carbs and protein while staying in ketosis, MCT keto diets have been employed to treat epilepsy. This is because long-chain triglycerides found in typical dietary fat, as opposed to MCTs, give more ketones for each gram of fat. Be aware that consuming MCTs primarily on their own might cause nausea and diarrhea. It's preferable to eat meals with a mix of MCTs & non-MCT fat to avoid this. Studies examining whether MCTs have broader advantages for weight reduction or blood sugar levels are lacking, however.

Calorie-restricted keto diet:

A calorie-restricted keto diet is identical to a regular ketogenic diet, with the exception that the number of calories is capped at a certain number. According to research, ketogenic diets are often effective whether or not calorie intake is controlled. This is due to the fact that consuming fat & being in a state of ketosis both have a satiating impact that tends to assist in avoiding overeating.

CKD (Cyclical Ketogenic Diet):

In the CKD diet, commonly referred to as carb back loading, days with increased carbohydrate intake are included, such as 5 keto days followed by 2 days with higher carb intake. The diet is designed for athletes who can utilize the days with more carbohydrates to replace muscle glycogen depleted after exercise.

TKD (Targeted Ketogenic Diet):

The TKD is comparable to a typical ketogenic diet, with the exception that carbs are eaten just before and after workouts. It is a middle ground between a traditional ketogenic diet & a cyclical keto diet which permits you to eat carbs on any day that you work out. It is based on the idea that since our muscles need more energy while we are active, carbohydrates ingested before or after an exertion will be absorbed much more effectively.

High Protein Keto Diet:

With a proportion of 35% protein, 60% fat, and 5% carbohydrates, this diet has more protein compared to a typical ketogenic diet. A high-protein ketogenic diet may help those who need to reduce weight, according to research. There isn't enough information to say if a long-term ketogenic diet has any health hazards similar to other types of ketogenic diets.

- **1.4 Overall Benefits**

The keto diet causes the body to run out of sugar stores, forcing it to burn fat for energy instead. Among other advantages, it could aid in weight loss, acne management, and heart health improvement. Using a ketogenic diet to control diabetes has several worthwhile advantages. According to research, being in nutritional ketosis significantly improves blood glucose regulation and promotes weight reduction. Some typical advantages offered include:

decreased reliance on drugs

Enhanced insulin sensitivity

blood pressure reduction

Typically, lowering cholesterol levels

Loss and maintenance of weight

The keto diet's potential to provide quick weight reduction is among its main benefits. Restricting carbohydrates to the degree where ketosis is attained results in both a significant reduction in body's fat content as well as an increase and retention of muscle mass. Low-carb, keto diets may lead to sustained, considerable weight loss, according to research. Those who are obese may shed an average of 15 kg in a year, according to Australian studies. This was 3 kg more than what was achieved during the study with the low-fat diet.

Blood sugar regulation:

The ability of the ketogenic diet to lower and maintain the level of blood sugar is the second main reason encouraging diabetic people to follow it. Carbohydrates are the macronutrient that substantially raises blood sugar levels. Ketogenic diets avoid major blood sugar increases because of their high carbohydrate limitation. Ketogenic diets have been shown in studies to be very successful in lowering HbA1c, a marker of long-term blood glucose management. A significant drop in levels of blood sugar and a betterment in control is also to be anticipated in people with other forms of diabetes, like type 1 diabetes & LADA. It should be noted that if blood glucose management improves and is maintained over a period of years, this may lower the risk of problems. Anybody on insulin should take care to avoid developing one. Consult your physician for assistance with this.

Lowering dependence on diabetic medications:

Ketogenic diets offer the added advantage of assisting persons with type 2 diabetes in lessening their reliance on diabetic medication since they are so successful at lowering blood sugar levels. In the Westman trial cited above, 95 percent of the participants were able to cut down on or entirely stop using their diabetic medications. When beginning a ketogenic diet, those using insulin and other medications that might cause hypos (such as sulphonylureas and glinides) may need to lower their dosage to avoid hypos. Consult your physician for guidance on this.

Insulin Insensitivity:

It has been shown that a ketogenic diet may help to restore insulin sensitivity since it targets the root cause of the insulin resistance that is an overabundance of insulin inside the body. This diet supports sustained lower insulin levels because reduced carbohydrate levels lead to lower levels of insulin. A diet high in carbs is like feeding insulin resistance gasoline. Diets high in carbohydrates result in a greater need for insulin, which makes insulin resistance worse. In contrast, since fat consumes the lowest amount of insulin of all the nutrients, a ketogenic diet reduces insulin levels. Reducing insulin levels also helps with fat burning since elevated levels of insulin prevent the breakdown of fat. As insulin levels drop over many hours, the body could start to break down fat cells.

Regulation of high blood pressure:

In the UK, 16 million individuals are thought to have excessive blood pressure. Heart disease, stroke, & kidney disease are just a few of the medical conditions that elevated blood pressure is associated with. It is also a feature of metabolic syndrome. A ketogenic diet has been shown in several trials to have the potential to decrease blood pressure in individuals with type 2 diabetes or obesity.

Amounts of cholesterol:

In general, cholesterol levels often decrease when on a ketogenic diet. It is advantageous when HDL cholesterol levels increase and LDL cholesterol levels fall. One of the most accurate measures of healthy cholesterol is the ratio of cholesterol to HDL. You may readily get this by dividing the cholesterol result by the HDL number. Your cholesterol is deemed healthy if the value is 3.5 or below. Research have indicated that this parameter of cholesterol health is often improved by the ketogenic diet.

Be aware that after beginning a keto diet, some patients may exhibit an increase in LDL and total cholesterol. This is often seen as a bad indicator, but if your entire cholesterol to HDL proportion is excellent, it may not necessarily mean that your heart health is becoming worse. If the cholesterol levels dramatically fluctuate while following a ketogenic diet, your physician is the ideal person to see for help since cholesterol is a difficult subject. You should get your cholesterol levels checked at least once a year in the UK so that any detrimental effects on cholesterol may be identified and treated as necessary.

Improved mental agility:

Some often-mentioned advantages of following a keto diet include mental clarity, an improvement in concentration, and superior memory. Increased consumption of omega-3-rich good fats, like those in fatty fish such as mackerel, tuna, and salmon, may enhance mood and cognitive function. This is due to the fact that omega-3 supplements boost the amount of a type of fatty acid known as DHA, which accounts for 15-30% of your brain. Long-term memory function is supported by the ketone beta-hydroxybutyrate synthesis.

Satiety:

Ketogenic diets have a beneficial effect on hunger. When the body becomes used to being in a state of ketosis, it adapts to getting its fuel from burning body fat, which may reduce appetite and cravings. They work well for:

minimizing desires

assisting you in maintaining satiety

lowering one's appetite for sweet meals

A ketogenic diet's ability to reduce body weight may assist in decreasing Leptin levels, which can then enhance Leptin sensitivity and increase satiety.

Candida:

Due to their ability to decrease blood sugar, which in turn lowers the amount of glucose excreted in the urine, ketogenic diets may help to lessen thrush and yeast infections. The urine contains glucose, which bacteria feed on and which creates a favorable environment for yeast & bacterial diseases. Moreover, it has been shown that consuming more lauric acid, a saturated fatty acid found in coconut oil is a key component of the ketogenic diet and has anti-microbial characteristics. It may assist with yeast infections and eradicate candida albicans.

- **1.5 Diabetes and it's Types**

People of all ages are susceptible to the prevalent disease known as diabetes. Diabetes comes in a variety of shapes. The most typical kind is type 2. You may control the illness to lead a healthy life & avoid consequences by using a variety of therapeutic methods. When your glucose level is too high, you get diabetes. It happens when your body doesn't process insulin effectively or when your pancreas doesn't produce any insulin at all. All ages are impacted by diabetes. Diabetes comes in a variety of types, most of which are chronic (lifelong) and treatable with medication and/or dietary modifications. Carbohydrates in your meals and beverages are the major source of glucose (sugar). It is the primary energy source for your body. All of the cells in your body get glucose from your blood to be used as fuel. When glucose is present in the bloodstream, it needs assistance—a "key"—to get to where it needs to go. Insulin is the key (a hormone). Glucose piles up in your system and results in high blood sugar if your pancreas doesn't produce enough insulin or if your body doesn't use it effectively (hyperglycemia).

Consistently high blood sugar levels over time may lead to health risks, including heart disease, nerve damage, and vision difficulties. Diabetes mellitus is the correct medical term for the condition. Diabetes insipidus is a different ailment that also goes by the name "diabetes," but they are not the same. Since they both result in increased thirst & frequent urination, they are both referred to as "diabetes". Unlike diabetes mellitus, diabetes insipidus is far less common.

Types of Diabetes:

Type 2 diabetes: In this type, the body either doesn't produce enough insulin or its cells don't react to it properly (insulin resistance). The most typical kind of diabetes is this one. While mostly affecting adults, it may also impact kids.

Prediabetes: This condition is a precursor to Type 2 diabetes. Your levels of blood glucose are above average but not strong enough to get a Type 2 diabetes diagnosis.

Type 1 diabetes: It is an autoimmune condition in which, for an unidentified cause, your immune system targets and kills insulin-making cells in your pancreas. Type 1 diabetes affects up to 10 percent of patients with the disease. While it may occur at any age, it is often diagnosed in children & young people.

Gestational diabetes: Some women experience the onset of this kind while pregnant. After pregnancy, gestational diabetes often disappears. The chance of acquiring Type 2 diabetes at a later age is increased if you've gestational diabetes, however.

Other forms of diabetes include:

Type 3c diabetes: It is a kind of diabetes that develops when your pancreas sustains an injury that impairs its capacity to make insulin (damage unrelated to autoimmune disease). Damage to the pancreas that results in diabetes may be brought on by pancreatic cancer, pancreatitis, cystic fibrosis, and hemochromatosis. Type 3c may also arise from having the pancreas removed (pancreatectomy).

LADA (Latent Autoimmune Diabetes in Adults): LADA is an autoimmune condition similar to Type 1 diabetes; however, it progresses considerably more slowly. Those who are identified with LADA are often older than 30.

Maturity-onset diabetes of young (MODY): Also known as monogenic diabetes, MODY is brought on by a hereditary genetic mutation that alters how your body produces and utilizes insulin. MODY now comes in more than ten distinct varieties. It affects up to five percent of patients with diabetes and usually runs in families.

Neonatal diabetes: During the first 6 months of life, this unusual type of diabetes develops. It also has a monogenic diabetes subtype. The lifelong type of neonatal diabetes known as persistent neonatal diabetes mellitus affects around 50% of newborns. The illness vanishes for another half after a few months of beginning, although it may recur later in life. Acute neonatal diabetes mellitus is the term used for this.

Brittle diabetes: It is a kind of Type one diabetes characterized by frequent, significant spikes and falls in blood sugar levels. Hospitalization is often a result of this instability. Rarely, brittle diabetes may need a pancreas transplant to be permanently treated.

- **1.6 Managing Diabetes - Role of Keto Diet**

The keto, or ketogenic, diet is very popular as a means to help individuals lose weight. But is it really a secure, efficient way to manage diabetes? The ketogenic diet is a high-fat, low-carb eating regimen. Most of what you consume is fat, whether that's unsaturated fats such as avocados, nuts, and seeds or saturated fats such as butter & coconut oil. Your diet contains lean or fatty proteins, which make up around 20% to 30% of your total calories (like bacon). Even foods that are normally regarded as healthful, such as whole grains, beans, milk, and a variety of fruits and vegetables, should be rigorously limited in terms of their carbohydrate content. Less than 50 g of carbohydrates per day are allowed on the ketogenic diet. In comparison, a medium apple contains 25 grams of carbohydrates.

Ketoacidosis vs ketosis:

Understanding the distinction between ketoacidosis & nutritional ketosis is crucial if you have diabetes. They both concern ketones. Yet, a severe condition known as ketoacidosis may develop when your body produces an excessive amount of ketones due to a lack of insulin. Excessive thirst, frequent urination, disorientation, and weakness or exhaustion are among the symptoms. Type 1 persons are more likely to experience it than Type 2 people. Compared to ketoacidosis, ketosis occurs at considerably lower and safer amounts of ketone bodies. In actuality, depending on the quantity of protein and carbohydrates you consume, this process occurs naturally throughout daily living. It is the condition that may cause weight reduction, particularly belly fat, and decrease A1C for many diabetics.

According to research, adopting a ketogenic diet may help persons with type 2 diabetes lose weight and control their blood sugar levels. In one research, type 2 diabetics who followed a year-long ketogenic diet lost weight, used less medication, and had a lower A1C. If you have insulin resistance, which is a condition in which your body doesn't react to the hormone insulin as it should, nutritional ketosis may be beneficial for you since it will reduce the amount of insulin your body needs and produces.

Little research has been done on the keto diet and types 1 diabetes. A1C levels were shown to be reduced in a short trial of persons with type 1 diabetes, but much more research is required to fully understand the diet's effects. Remember that the majority of research has only examined the short-term effects of the ketogenic diet. It is unknown whether it is a reliable method for managing diabetes over the long run. Be warned that sticking to the keto diet may be challenging if you choose to give it a try. For many individuals, the plan's very low carbohydrate intake marks a significant adjustment. Also, it could make you feel exhausted for some weeks as your body adjusts. Making a meal plan that you can stick to with keto-friendly foods and ready-to-eat snacks is a fantastic idea to ensure success.

Is Keto Safe for Diabetic Patients?

Your kind of diabetes will determine this. Obese type 2 patients often tend to get excellent outcomes safely. It's essential to see your doctor first if you've type 1 diabetes and wish to attempt the ketogenic diet. You must keep a close eye on your health and look out for ketoacidosis symptoms. Working closely with the doctor is a good idea for any kind since you might need to switch up your prescription.

- **1.7 Boosting Immune System**

The ability of the ketogenic diet to promote the development of gamma & delta T cells in the mice's lungs is thought to be the source of the diet's defensive effects. This encourages the epithelial cells lining the nose channel to produce more mucus, which traps and expels the infection. The benefits of keto are not only confined to weight loss; they may also help prevent certain illnesses. A ketogenic diet has been shown to be an effective way to raise your immunity and fight flu symptoms. According to an ongoing study, the ketogenic diet may prevent the spread of the new coronavirus by retaining the influenza virus.

The research also revealed that cells that adhere to a ketogenic diet improve mucus formation, which shields the body against the flu and its unpleasant side effects.

According to the study, following a Keto diet can even help the body become more resistant to some viral diseases.

Previous reports have claimed to have found some indications that the Ketogenic diet may help prevent the organization of inflammasomes that are harmful to our immune system and adversely stimulate it.

There are many ways that the ketogenic diet exerts its anticonvulsant effects:

Increased levels of ketone bodies, such as -hydroxybutyrate, have shown to be protective against damage from reactive oxygen species. Therefore the keto diet also has anti-cancerous properties.

The anti-seizure properties of the keto diet may also alter the equilibrium of GABA structures, limiting autophagy. Moreover, its antiepileptic effects could be connected to improved excitatory energy transfer. As a result, it is reported to partially treat epilepsy.

The ketogenic diet reduces inflammation in the body. Inflammation is intimately related to gut health.

Infectious particles may get past the gut barrier when your gut isn't working properly, which signals the immune system to start working, which is definitely not a permanent resistant response.

Increased generation of intestinal stem cells was linked to higher levels of ketones. The pathogenic gut bacteria's favorite food, sugar, is also denied to them by the keto diet.

- **1.8 Tips for Maximizing Keto Diet Results**

Keto is a distinct kind of dietary regimen. By combining the benefits of nutritional ketosis with the efficiency of calorie tracking, it offers people a potent strategy for shedding weight and improving overall health.

Get rid of non-Keto goods from your cupboard.

A healthy atmosphere is essential for bringing about any long-lasting transformation. Getting rid of everything that doesn't match your low-carb diet as a terrific first step. It requires getting rid of sugary snacks and treats (along with beans, grains, and flour if the entire family is going Keto). Eliminate temptations, and you'll make things a lot simpler in the long-run for yourself.

Stock your cupboard with basic Keto items.

A good time to start over and restock on Keto essentials is when you're cleaning up your home. If you purchase in quantity, it's also a fantastic way to save your time & money. Healthy Keto components that are often utilized include:

Kale, broccoli, spinach, zucchini, asparagus, and cauliflower, either frozen or fresh.

Grass-fed meats, eggs, poultry, fish, tofu (if vegetarian or vegan), & dairy are all good sources of protein (if tolerated).

Good fats include avocado, almonds, seeds, olive oil, coconut oil, and milk.

Herbs, spices, & natural sweeteners (low-carb) like stevia are used as sweeteners and flavors.

Simple Keto meal planning can help you stay on schedule and organized.

If you have a well-thought-out strategy in place and a mechanism to monitor your progress, it's often a lot simpler to thrive with a new habit. Based on personal preferences, you may make a customized meal plan & shopping list.

Get to know these bread options for Keto flour (and desserts)

Contrary to common opinion, following a ketogenic diet doesn't need you to permanently give up scrumptious bread and baked products. Coconut & almond flour is going to become 2 of your new closest friends if you haven't already met them.

Load up on your Keto-friendly favorite sides and condiments for a flavorful touch.

Use Keto-friendly condiments, dressings, and side dishes to quickly add a touch of flavor to the meals and prevent your ketogenic diet from becoming too restrictive:

Avoid non-Keto sections at the grocery store to avoid temptation.

Try staying around the edges of the store where the majority of the fresh fruit is located if you find yourself being drawn in by the colorful wrapping of processed foods inside the dessert aisles. Whenever possible, choose local markets. If it doesn't work, you might try ordering produce in bulk online or via home delivery boxes.

Establishing habits will help you overcome the need for willpower.

Willpower is a scarce resource. Thus, you have to maintain it as much as you can. In order to accomplish this, it might be helpful to establish routines and habits that make your new action automatic.

CHAPTER 2:
Keto Diet - Breakfast Recipes

1. Green Eggs

Ready in: 20 mins.
Serves: 2
Difficulty: easy
Ingredients:

- 2 leeks (trimmed), sliced
- 1 ½ tbsp. of olive oil, plus some extra oil
- 2 cloves of garlic, sliced
- ½ tsp. of fennel seeds
- ½ tsp. of coriander seeds
- Some chili flakes, plus some extra to serve
- 2 eggs, large
- 200g of spinach
- 1 tsp. of lemon
- 2 tbsp. of Greek yogurt

Directions:

- In a big frying pan, heat the oil. Add the leeks & some salt, and cook till soft. Garlic, coriander, fennel, and chili flakes should be added. Turn the heat down and add the spinach after the seeds start to crackle. Once the spinach has wilted & decreased, scrape it to one side of the pan and continue to stir everything together. Crack the eggs into the pan, add a little oil, and fry until done to your preference.
- Season the spinach mixture after incorporating the yogurt. To serve, pile onto 2 plates, top with one fried egg, pour some lemon juice over it, and season with salt, pepper, and red pepper flakes.

Nutritional values per serving:
Total Calories: 298 kcal, **Fat:** 20g, **Carbohydrates:** 8g, **Protein:** 18g

2. Breakfast Omelette Roll-Up

Ready in: 15 mins.
Serves: 1
Difficulty: easy
Ingredients:

- Some olive or rapeseed oil for frying

- 1 egg (large)
- 1 tbsp. of fresh coriander
- 2 tbsp. of tomato salsa

Directions:

- With 1 tablespoon of water, beat the egg. In a medium nonstick pan, heat the oil. After adding the egg, swirl it over the pan's bottom as if cooking a pancake. Cook the egg until it has been set. It doesn't need to be turned.
- Roll up the pancake after carefully placing it on a board, spreading it with salsa and garnishing it with coriander. You may store it in the fridge for two days and eat it either warm or cold.

Nutritional values per serving:
Total Calories: 133kcal, **Fat:** 10g, **Carbohydrates:** 2g, **Protein:** 9g

3. Pancakes

Ready in: 25 mins.
Serves: 2
Difficulty: easy
Ingredients:

- 75ml of almond milk
- 4 eggs
- 1 tsp. of stevia
- Some ground cinnamon
- 1 tsp. of baking powder
- ½ tsp. of vanilla extract
- 175g of almond flour

Directions:

- In a dish, combine the eggs & almond milk. Stir to blend after adding the baking powder, stevia, cinnamon, almond flour, and vanilla.
- A frying pan should be heated to medium-low. Add a few teaspoons of the batter & cook for two to three minutes or until the edges are firm. When golden, flip & cook for an additional 2 minutes. Repeat with the rest of the batter, then serve it in stacks with your preferred garnishes.

Nutritional values per serving:
Total Calories: 731kcal, **Fat:** 61g, **Carbohydrates:** 7g, **Protein:** 38g

4. Masala Frittata & Avocado Salsa

Ready in: 40 mins.
Serves: 4
Difficulty: easy
Ingredients:

- 3 onions, 2 & ½ thinly sliced & half finely chopped
- 2 tbsp. of olive oil
- 1 tbsp. of Madras curry paste
- 1 deseeded red chili, finely chopped
- 500g of halved cherry tomatoes
- tiny pack of coriander, roughly chopped

- 1 stoned avocado, peeled & cubed
- 8 eggs (large), beaten
- juice of 1 lemon

Directions:

- A medium nonstick, oven-safe frying pan should be heated with oil. Add the sliced onions & simmer for approximately 10 minutes or until they are tender and golden. Fry for a further minute after adding the Madras paste before adding half the tomatoes & half the chilies. Cook the mixture until it thickens and all of the tomatoes explode.
- The grill should be quite hot. Pour over the hot onion mixture after seasoning the eggs with half the coriander. Cook for 8 to 10 minutes at low heat, stirring occasionally, until the mixture is nearly set. After set, transfer it to the grill for 3–5 minutes.
- To prepare the salsa, combine the avocado, remaining tomatoes, remaining coriander, remaining onion, and remaining lemon juice. Season to taste & serve with a frittata.

Nutritional values per serving:
Total Calories: 347kcal, **Fat:** 25g, **Carbohydrates:** 12g, **Protein:** 16g

5. Courgette Frittatas

Ready in: 45 mins.
Serves: 2
Difficulty: easy
Ingredients:

- 4 spring onions
- 2 small or 1 large courgettes
- 2 tsp. of avocado oil
- 3 eggs (large)
- 1 garlic clove, crushed
- 4 tbsp. of Greek yogurt
- good pinch of dill fronds

Directions:

- Place an empty muffin tray inside the preheated oven at 220°C/200°F fan/gas 7 levels. Grate one big or two tiny courgettes coarsely, then slice four spring onions. The spring onions should be fried for around three minutes in a frying pan with 2 tsp. of rapeseed oil. Cook for a further minute after stirring in the shredded courgette and one smashed garlic clove. Then, leave it aside to cool.
- In a jug, combine 3 big eggs, a fair pinch of dill fronds, and 4 tablespoons of Greek yogurt. Season to taste. Add the combination of the courgettes. Remove the muffin tray from the oven, add eight muffin liners, divide the mixture of egg among them, & bake for 15 to 18 minutes, or until the tops are firm and golden. Serve a salad with it warm or cold.

Nutritional values per serving:
Total Calories: 311kcal, **Fat:** 22g, **Carbohydrates:** 8g, **Protein:** 20g

6. Mushroom, Ham & Spinach Frittata

Ready in: 15 mins.
Serves: 2
Difficulty: easy
Ingredients:

- 80g of sliced chestnut mushrooms

- 1 tsp. of oil
- 50g of ham, diced
- 4 eggs (medium), beaten
- 80g bag of spinach
- 1 tbsp. of grated cheddar

Directions:

- Turn the grill's heat to the maximum setting. An oven-safe frying pan with medium-high heat is used to heat the oil. Add the mushrooms and cook for two minutes or until they are mostly soft. Cook for a further minute, stirring in the ham & spinach, or till the spinach has wilted. Add a good amount of salt and black pepper for seasoning.
- Pour all over the eggs after lowering the heat. Uninterrupted cooking for 3 minutes till the eggs are almost set. Place the cheese on top and cook for two minutes. Serve warm or cool.

Nutritional values per serving:
Total Calories: 226kcal, **Fat:** 15g, **Carbohydrates:** 0g, **Protein:** 22g

7. Crustless Quiche

Ready in: 55 mins.
Serves: 6
Difficulty: easy
Ingredients:

- 1 finely chopped onion
- 20g of butter, plus some extra for tin
- 100g of smoked bacon or pancetta, chopped
- 8 eggs (large)
- 200g of broccoli or asparagus, trimmed
- 80g of parmesan cheese or gruyere
- 150ml of double cream

Directions:

- Heat the oven up to 180°C/160°F fan/gas 4. A 23 cm round deep springform cake pan should be buttered and lined so that the paper extends 2-3 cm over the tin's edges.
- Butter should be melted in a pan. For 10 minutes or until the onion & pancetta are tender and translucent, add the ingredients and simmer over low heat.
- Bring to a boil some water that has been mildly seasoned. Cut broccoli florets into tiny pieces; leave asparagus intact. Let the vegetables steam-dry after 2 minutes of boiling, then drain.

Nutritional values per serving:
Total Calories: 401kcal, **Fat:** 34g, **Carbohydrates:** 3g, **Protein:** 19g

8. Olive & Basil Eggs

Ready in: 15 mins.
Serves: 3
Difficulty: easy
Ingredients:

- ½ pack of basil (small)
- 3 eggs (large)
- 6 Kalamata olives, pitted
- 1 tsp. of cider vinegar
- 1 tbsp. of olive oil

Directions:

- Eggs should be boiled for 8 minutes and then cooled in cold water. Halve after peeling. Scoop the yolks out.

- In a small bowl, combine the olives, basil, oil, vinegar, and some freshly ground pepper. Using a hand blender, puree briefly before adding the yolk and coarsely combining. Refill the eggs with the mixture, then refrigerate.

Nutritional values per serving:
Total Calories: 137kcal, **Fat:** 12g, **Carbohydrates:** 0g, **Protein:** 10g

9. Mushroom, Tarragon & Sausage Frittata

Ready in: 20 mins.
Serves: 2
Difficulty: easy
Ingredients:

- 200g of sliced chestnut mushrooms
- 1 tbsp. of olive oil
- 2 pork sausages
- 100g of fine asparagus
- 1 clove of garlic, crushed
- 3 eggs (large)
- 1 tbsp. of whole-grain mustard
- 2 tbsp. of soured cream, half-fat
- Rocket salad (mixed), to serve (optional)
- 1 tbsp. of chopped tarragon

Directions:

- Heat your grill to high. In a medium-sized nonstick frying pan, heat the oil. Add the mushrooms, and cook for 3 minutes on high heat. Squeeze the sausage meat into nuggets and add to the pan. Fry for 5 minutes further or until golden brown. Cook the asparagus and garlic together for a further minute.
- In a jug, combine the soured cream, eggs, mustard, and tarragon. After thoroughly seasoning, add the egg mixture to the pan. Sauté for 3–4 minutes, then grill for an additional 1–2 minutes, or until the top is just starting to set with some wobbling in the center. If desired, serve with salad greens.

Nutritional values per serving:
Total Calories: 433kcal, **Fat:** 32g, **Carbohydrates:** 8g, **Protein:** 25g

10. Avocado & Bacon Frittata

Ready in: 35 mins.
Serves: 4
Difficulty: easy
Ingredients:

- 3 tbsp. of olive oil
- 8 rashers streaky bacon, smoked
- 6 beaten eggs
- 1 red chili (small), finely chopped
- 1 avocado (large), halved, peeled, stoned & cut in chunky slices
- 1 heaped tsp. of Dijon mustard
- 200g bag of salad leaves, mixed
- 2 tsp. of red wine vinegar
- 12 halved baby plum tomatoes

Directions:

- The bacon rashers should be fried until fully cooked and crisp in batches over high heat in a 24 cm nonstick ovenproof pan that has been preheated. Break the other four into big pieces and coarsely chop the other 4. Clean the pan, then set it aside onto kitchen paper.
- Heat your grill to high. In the pan, heat 1 tbsp of oil. After seasoning,

place the eggs into the skillet along with the bacon. Cook for about 8 minutes, or until nearly set, on low heat. Place the bacon bits and avocado slices on top. Grill quickly for 4 minutes or until set.

Nutritional values per serving:
Total Calories: 467kcal, **Fat:** 38g, **Carbohydrates:** 7g, **Protein:** 22g

11. Kale & Mushroom brunch

Ready in: 20 mins.
Serves: 4
Difficulty: easy
Ingredients:

- 1 clove of garlic
- 250g of mushrooms
- 1 tbsp. of olive oil
- 4 eggs
- 160g bag of kale

Directions:

- Cut the mushrooms into slices and mince the garlic. In a large nonstick frying pan that has been heated with olive oil, cook the garlic for one minute. When the mushrooms are tender, add them. Add the kale next. If the kale won't fit completely in the pan, put half of it and stir until it wilts. Then add the remaining kale. Season once all of the kale has wilted.
- The eggs should now be cracked in and gently cooked for two to three minutes. After the eggs are done to your preference, continue cooking them for another 2 to 3 minutes under the lid. Serve with normal or keto bread.

Nutritional values per serving:
Total Calories: 154kcal, **Fat:** 1g, **Carbohydrates:** 1g, **Protein:** 13g

12. Scrambled Eggs with Spinach, Basil & Tomatoes

Ready in: 10 mins.
Serves: 2
Difficulty: easy
Ingredients:

- 3 halved tomatoes
- 1 tbsp. of olive oil, plus one tsp.
- 4 eggs (large)
- ⅓ pack of basil (small), chopped
- 4 tbsp. of natural bio yogurt
- 175g of baby spinach, well dried

Directions:

- In a large nonstick frying pan that has been heated with 1 tsp. of oil, add the tomatoes & sauté them cut-side down over medium heat. Beat the eggs with yogurt, 2 tablespoons of water, a good amount of black pepper, and the basil in a jug while the potatoes are boiling.

- To serve, place the tomatoes on plates. When the eggs are cooking, add the spinach into the pan and let it wilt while tossing it occasionally.
- In a nonstick pan with the remaining oil heated over medium heat, add the egg mixture & cook, stirring occasionally, until scrambled & just set. Place a serving of spinach on each dish, then top with scrambled eggs

Nutritional values per serving:
Total Calories: 297kcal, **Fat:** 20g, **Carbohydrates:** 10g, **Protein:** 20g

13. Herby Omelette

Ready in: 10 mins.
Serves: 2
Difficulty: easy
Ingredients:

- 3 halved tomatoes
- 1 tsp. of olive oil
- 4 eggs (large)
- 1 tbsp. of chopped basil
- 1 tbsp. of chopped parsley

Directions:

- The tomatoes should be cooked cut-side down in hot oil into a small nonstick frying pan until they begin to soften and turn color. Beat the eggs in a mixing bowl while adding lots of black pepper and herbs.
- Place the tomatoes on two serving dishes after scooping them out of the pan. Pour the mixture of egg into the pan & gently swirl with a spoon to allow the uncooked egg to run into the space created by the moving of the egg that has set on the pan's base. When it is almost done cooking, stop stirring to let it set in an omelet. Serve with tomatoes after cutting them into four pieces.

Nutritional values per serving:
Total Calories: 204kcal, **Fat:** 14g, **Carbohydrates:** 4g, **Protein:** 17g

14. Pancetta Avocado Soldiers With Soft-Boiled Eggs

Ready in: 15 mins.
Serves: 2
Difficulty: easy
Ingredients:

- 1 tbsp. of avocado oil
- 4 eggs
- 100g of pancetta rashers, smoked
- 1 avocado (ripe), cut into slices

Directions:

- Bring to a boil a large pot of salted water. Eggs should be carefully placed in the water and boiled for 5 minutes to get runny yolks.
- Each avocado slice should be wrapped with pancetta while the oil is heating in a nonstick pan. Cook and crisp for 1-2 minutes in a high-heat frying pan.
- Eggs should be served in egg cups with avocado soldiers onto the side for dipping.

Nutritional values per serving:
Total Calories: 517kcal, **Fat:** 46g, **Carbohydrates:** 1g, **Protein:** 22g

15. Spinach and Sprout Baked Eggs

Ready in: 50 mins.
Serves: 4
Difficulty: easy
Ingredients:

- 1 tsp. of cumin seeds
- 1 tbsp. of olive oil
- 1 chopped onion
- 1 chopped green chili
- 2 cloves of garlic, crushed
- 300g of roughly shredded Brussels sprouts
- Half lemon, juiced
- 450g of spinach
- 6 eggs
- ½ small pack of coriander, sriracha, yogurt and keto bread or sourdough (thick slices) to serve

Directions:

- In a pan with the high sides over medium heat, spread the cumin seeds & lightly toast them. Next, add the onion & cook for about 5 minutes or until tender. For one minute, add the garlic & chili. Add the spinach to the sprouts after cooking for 5 minutes to soften them; you may need to do it in batches. Sauté the spinach until it has wilted, then add lemon juice to taste. Properly season.
- To make the six holes in greens for the eggs, use a spoon. Eggs should be cracked into the holes in the pan, covered with a lid, and cooked for 5 to 7 minutes until the whites are set, but the yolks are still runny. Coriander should be added last. Serve right away with sourdough and sriracha-drizzled natural yogurt.

Nutritional values per serving:
Total Calories: 268kcal, **Fat:** 15g, **Carbohydrates:** 10g, **Protein:** 21g

16. Bun-less Egg, Bacon & Cheese

Ready in: 15 mins.
Serves: 1
Difficulty: easy
Ingredients:

- 2 tbsp. of water
- 2 eggs (large)
- 1/2 lightly mashed avocado
- 1/4 cup of shredded cheddar
- 1 slice of bacon (cooked), halved

Directions:

- 2 Mason jar lids should be placed on a nonstick pan (centers removed). Cooking spray the whole pan, then set it over medium heat. To break up the yolk, crack eggs in the middle of the lids and softly stir with a fork.
- Pour water across lids & cover pan. Cook eggs while letting them steam for approximately 3 minutes or until the whites are fully cooked. Remove the cover, then add some cheddar to one egg. Sauté for another minute or so or until cheese begins to melt gently.
- Onto a platter, invert an egg bun without the cheese. Add fried bacon and mashed avocado as garnish.

Place the cheese-side-down cheesy egg bun on top.

Nutritional values per serving:
Total Calories: 463kcal, **Fat:** 37g, **Carbohydrates:** 3g, **Protein:** 24g

17. Cinnamon Rolls

Ready in: 1hr. 20 mins.
Serves: 1
Difficulty: easy
Ingredients:
For rolls:

- 2 tbsp. of coconut flour
- 2 cups of almond flour, finely ground
- 1/4 cup of granulated sugar
- 2 eggs (large)
- 1 tbsp. of baking powder, gluten-free
- 2 tsp. of vanilla extract (pure)
- 4 oz. of cream cheese
- 2 cups of shredded mozzarella
- 3 tbsp. of butter, divided, melted, plus some more for brushing
- 1 tbsp. of ground cinnamon
- 1/3 cup of packed brown sugar

For Glaze:

- 2 tbsp. of heavy cream
- 3 oz. of cream cheese
- 2 tsp. of granulated sugar

Directions:

- To make the rolls, mix the baking powder, granulated Swerve, almond flour, and coconut flour in a big bowl. Eggs and vanilla are whisked in a different bowl.
- Melt the mozzarella & cream cheese in the microwave, stirring after every 30 seconds, for approximately 90 seconds. To the dry mixture, add the egg mixture and the cheese mixture that has been melted and blend thoroughly.
- Turn out the dough onto a piece of parchment paper that has been placed on a work surface. Roll the parchment till it is 16" x 10", and place another sheet on top. Drizzle 2 tablespoons of melted butter over the dough before topping it with cinnamon and brown sugar.
- Set the oven up to 375 degrees. Using parchment paper and butter, line an 8" × 8" metal baking pan. Make a log out of the dough by starting at the long end. Ten minutes of cooling.
- Place the log in the baking dish after cutting it into 12 equal pieces. Roll tops should be brushed with the last tablespoon of heated butter.
- Bake for approximately 30 minutes or until the rolls are brown. Let to cool a little.
- Make the frosting in the meantime: Melt cream cheese in a small heat-proof bowl. Swerve and heavy cream should be blended well.
- Before serving, drizzle frosting over the heated buns.

Nutritional values per serving:
Total Calories: 311kcal, **Fat:** 24g, **Carbohydrates:** 12g, **Protein:** 11g

18. Egg, Ham & Cheese Roll-Ups

Ready in: 35 mins.
Serves: 10
Difficulty: easy

Ingredients:

- 2 tsp. of garlic powder
- 10 eggs (large)
- Kosher salt
- 2 tbsp. of butter
- Black Pepper, Freshly ground
- 1 1/2 cups of shredded cheddar
- 1 cup of chopped tomatoes
- 1 cup of baby spinach
- 20 slices of ham

Directions:

- Heat the broiler. Crack eggs into a large bowl. Salt and pepper to taste, then whisk in the garlic powder.
- Melt butter in a big nonstick pan over medium heat. Add the eggs and scramble for three minutes, stirring periodically. After the cheddar has melted, toss in the tomatoes and baby spinach until well incorporated.
- Two ham slices should be placed on a cutting board. Add a generous scoop of scrambled eggs on top, then wrap up. Repeat with the remaining eggs and ham.
- Put the roll-ups into a shallow baking tray and broil for 5 minutes or until the ham is crispy.

Nutritional values per serving:
Total Calories: 258kcal, **Fat:** 18g, **Carbohydrates:** 3g, **Protein:** 20g

19. Pumpkin Pie

Ready in: 3hrs. 30 mins.
Serves: 16
Difficulty: easy
Ingredients:
For crust:

- 3 tbsp. of coconut flour
- 1 1/2 cups of almond flour
- 1/4 tsp. of baking powder
- 4 tbsp. of butter, melted
- 1/4 tsp. of kosher salt
- 1 egg (large), beaten

For filling:

- 1 cup of heavy cream
- 1 can of pumpkin puree (15 oz.)
- 1/2 cup of packed brown sugar
- 1 tsp. of ground cinnamon
- 3 eggs (large), beaten
- 1/2 tsp. of ground ginger
- 1/4 tsp. of ground cloves
- 1/4 tsp. of ground nutmeg
- 1/4 tsp. of kosher salt
- Whipped cream, to serve (optional)
- 1 tsp. of pure vanilla extract

Directions:

- Set the oven up to 350 degrees. Mix the almond flour, baking soda, coconut flour, and salt in a big basin. Stir in the egg and melted butter till a dough forms. After properly pressing the dough into a 9" pie pan, prick the crust all over with a fork.
- Bake for 10 minutes or until gently browned.
- Pumpkin, brown sugar, cream, eggs, spices, & vanilla should all be well combined in a big basin. Fill crust with pumpkin filling and partially bake.
- Bake for 45 to 50 minutes, or until top is brown and the center of filling is somewhat jiggly.
- Turn off the oven and hold the door open. The pie should be chilled until it is time to serve after cooling in the oven for an hour.

- If desired, eat with whipped cream.

Nutritional values per serving:
Total Calories: 193kcal, **Fat:** 15g, **Carbohydrates:** 8g, **Protein:** 5g

20. Almond Flour Crepes

Ready in: 30 mins.
Serves: 16
Difficulty: easy
Ingredients:
Base crepes:

- 1 cup of Water (divided)
- 2 tbsp. of Gelatin powder
- 1 cup of Almond Flour
- 4 Eggs (large)
- 1/4 tsp. of Sea salt (increase to half tsp. for savory)
- 2 tbsp. of Ghee (melted)

Optional:

- 1/2 tsp. of Vanilla extract

Directions:

- Add gelatin and 1/2 cup water to a small bowl. Let to blossom for 3 minutes.
- In the meanwhile, whisk the remaining half cup water, eggs, melted coconut oil or ghee, sea salt, almond flour, and optional additions (if using). Once smooth, blend.
- Blend the gelatin mixture in a blender until it is completely smooth. Add a bit of additional water to thin down excessively thick batter if making crepes. (Avoid being excessively skinny. The batter could still be a touch thicker than usual.)
- An 8-inch greased pan should be heated over low heat. In order to distribute the batter uniformly into a thin layer, swiftly turn the pan in a circle several times after adding 1/4 cup of batter. (At first, there could be empty air bubbles; keep spinning, & the batter would fill them up.) Ideally, you can complete 2-3 revolutions. After the sides are dry, cook for 1 to 2 minutes more before gently flipping and cooking for a further minute onto the other side.
- Continue by using the remaining batter.

Nutritional values per serving:
Total Calories: 125kcal, **Fat:** 10g, **Carbohydrates:** 2g, **Protein:** 6g

21. Chaffle

Ready in: 10 mins.
Serves: 2
Difficulty: easy
Ingredients:

- 1 Egg (large)
- 1/2 cup of Mozzarella cheese (shredded)
- 2 tbsp. of Almond Flour (or 2 tsp. of coconut flour)
- 1/2 tsp. of Psyllium husk powder
- 1/3 cup of Grated Parmesan cheese
- 1/2 cup of Mozzarella cheese (shredded)
- 1 Egg (large)
- 1/2 tsp. of Italian seasoning
- 1 clove of Garlic (minced; or you can use half clove)
- 1/4 tsp. of Baking powder

Directions:

- Your little waffle maker should be heated up for about five minutes.

- All the components for the chaffle batter are combined (everything except the toppings, if any)
- Put just enough pancake batter in the waffle machine to completely cover the surface. (With a standard waffle maker, that amounts to roughly 1/2 cup of batter; for a little waffle maker, 1/4 cup.)
- Sauté for approximately 3 to 4 minutes or until browned and crispy.
- Remove from the waffle machine with care, then place it aside to continue to crisp up. (Cooling helps with texture.) Repeat if there is any leftover batter.

Nutritional values per serving:
Total Calories: 208kcal, **Fat:** 16g, **Carbohydrates:** 4g, **Protein:** 11g

22. Almond Flour Waffles

Ready in: 15 mins.
Serves: 2
Difficulty: easy
Ingredients:

- 1/2 cup of Almond Flour
- 1 Egg (large), separated
- 1/4 tsp. of Sea salt
- 1/2 tsp. of Baking powder
- 2 tbsp. of Almond butter
- 1/4 cup of Un-sweetened almond milk
- 2 tbsp. of Unsalted butter
- 1/2 tsp. of Vanilla extract

Directions:

- The waffle maker should be preheated. Lightly grease.
- In the meanwhile, whip the egg whites in a small bowl with a hand mixer until firm peaks form. Set aside.
- Almond flour, baking soda, and salt should all be combined in a large basin. Set aside.
- Melt the butter & almond butter in a small dish in the microwave or a saucepan over low heat. Add the mixture of butter to dry flour bowl after whisking it together.
- The batter should now include almond milk, yolk, and vanilla. Until smooth, stir.
- With the batter, fold your egg whites in. Mix just enough to prevent pockets of whites from remaining distinct from the remaining batter, being cautious not to overly denature the whites. The batter ought to be frothy and airy.
- Pour half of the batter into the waffle maker that has been lightly oiled. Shut the lid and cook for 5 minutes or until the steam stops pouring out. To make it simpler, take the waffle from the waffle iron, unplug it and allow it to cool somewhat. When it transitions from hot to warm, it will become crisp. Continue by using the remaining batter.

Nutritional values per serving:
Total Calories: 401kcal, **Fat:** 37g, **Carbohydrates:** 9g, **Protein:** 13g

23. Granola Cereal

Ready in: 25 mins.
Serves: 12
Difficulty: easy
Ingredients:

- 1 cup of Hazelnuts

- 1 cup of Almonds
- 1 cup of Pecans
- 1/3 cup of Sunflower seeds
- 1/3 cup of Pumpkin seeds
- 6 tbsp. of Besti Erythritol
- 1 Egg white (large)
- 1/2 cup of flax seed meal
- 1 tsp. of Vanilla extract
- 1/4 cup of unsalted butter (measured solid and then melted)

Directions:

- Set the oven up to 325 degrees Fahrenheit (163 degrees C). Use parchment paper to line one big baking sheet or two smaller ones.
- Grind almonds & hazelnuts in a food processor periodically until the majority of the nuts are chopped into big bits.
- Add pecans. Pulse once more, stopping as the pecans are broken up into big chunks.
- Add the golden flaxseed meal, erythritol, sunflower seeds, pumpkin seeds, and sunflower seeds. Just pulse enough to combine everything thoroughly. Avoid over-processing! The majority of the seeds must be whole, and there should be a good number of nut bits still present.
- Fill the food processor with the egg white. Pour it in as well after equally combining the melted butter & vanilla extract into a small dish.
- Pulse a few times, use a spatula to stir a bit from the base to the top, and then pulse a few times more. Repeat as necessary to ensure that everything is uniformly covered. Remind yourself not to over-process. You should have a mixture of coarse grain and nut bits at the conclusion of this phase, and the egg white & butter should have slightly moistened everything.
- Put the nut mixture in a single layer to the prepped baking sheet and flatten the mixture into a thin rectangle that is between 1/4 and 1/3 inch (.6 and.8 cm) thick. Bake for 15 to 18 minutes, until just golden, paying careful attention to the edges.
- Before chopping into pieces, let cool fully. As you take the granola out of the oven, it will be mushy; but as it cools, it will become crisp.

Nutritional values per serving:
Total Calories: 278kcal, **Fat:** 26g, **Carbohydrates:** 7g, **Protein:** 7g

24. Egg Muffins

Ready in: 45 mins.
Serves: 12
Difficulty: easy
Ingredients:

- 1 cup of Cauliflower (cut in half-inch florets)
- 1 cup of Broccoli (cut in half-inch florets)
- 1 cup of chopped Red bell pepper (in half-inch pieces)
- 2 tbsp. of Olive oil
- 2 cloves of Garlic
- 8 Eggs (large)
- 1 tsp. of Sea salt
- 1/4 cup of Heavy cream

- 3/4 cup of shredded Cheddar cheese (replace it with veggies if you want dairy-free)
- 1/2 tsp. of Black pepper

Directions:

- Set the oven up to 400 degrees Fahrenheit (204 degrees C). Cover the baking sheet with foil or parchment paper (grease it if using foil).
- Combine the broccoli, red pepper, cauliflower, garlic powder, and olive oil in a big bowl.
- On the baking sheet, arrange the veggies in a single layer. Roast broccoli in the prepared oven for 15 to 20 minutes or until the edges are browned.
- In the meanwhile, arrange a muffin pan with 12 silicone or parchment muffin liners.
- Keep your oven on once the veggies are done. Place the vegetables in the muffin tins in an equal layers.
- Black pepper, sea salt, and heavy cream are all whisked together. Add the cheddar cheese and stir. Over the veggies in the muffin cups, pour the egg mixture.
- Bake the eggs for 15 to 20 minutes or until they are set.

Nutritional values per serving:
Total Calories: 124kcal, **Fat:** 10g, **Carbohydrates:** 2g, **Protein:** 6g

25. Cheddar Broccoli Quiche

Ready in: 50 mins.
Serves: 6
Difficulty: easy

Ingredients:

For pie crust:

- 1 pie crust (Almond flour)

For broccoli:

- 2 cloves of Garlic (minced)
- 1 tbsp. of Olive oil
- 1/4 cup of Water
- 2 cups of Broccoli (in small florets)

For filling:

- 1/3 cup of Heavy cream
- 5 Eggs (large)
- 1/2 tsp. of Sea salt
- 1 cup of shredded Cheddar cheese
- 1/4 tsp. of Black pepper

Directions:

- Make the pie crust made with almond flour as directed. Before adding the filling, let it cool for 15 minutes at least. Keep your oven on at 177 °C (350 ° f).
- Using the quantities listed in the ingredients, sauté the broccoli & garlic. Quiche may be quicker since the florets are smaller. Cool until no longer hot, at least for ten minutes.
- In a big bowl, whisk together the cream, eggs, salt, & pepper. Add 1 cup, i.e., 113 g of grated cheese.
- In the pie crust, arrange the broccoli. Next, evenly distribute the cheese and pour the mixture of eggs over it. To protect the crust's edges, use foil or a pie crust protector. Keep the filler exposed.
- Bake until set for 30-35 minutes. Chill before slicing for 10 to 20 minutes.

Nutritional values per serving:
Total Calories: 573kcal, **Fat:** 51g, **Carbohydrates:** 13g, **Protein:** 23g

26. Breakfast Yogurt

Ready in: 15 mins.
Serves: 8
Difficulty: easy
Ingredients:

- 2 cups of Water
- 1/4 cup of Almonds
- 2 cups of Heavy cream
- 1/2 tbsp. of Gelatin powder
- 2 Probiotic (active cultures) capsules

For toppings:

- Almonds, sliced
- Eaton Hemp Hearts
- Coconut chips
- Jam, sugar-free
- Berries (blueberries, raspberries, strawberries)

Directions:

- 2 16-oz jars should be cleaned under hot, soapy water. Dry, then put aside.
- Put the almond milk & cream into a medium-sized saucepan over medium to low heat. For 5-7 minutes, heat slowly, stirring regularly, until bubbles start to appear at the rims. (Time might vary greatly depending on the kind of pan you use). Avoid boiling or simmering.
- Gelatin should be strewn over the saucepan, don't spill it, and whisk until it dissolves.
- Remove from heat.
- Fill the sterilized jars with the cream mixture. Let the mixture cool to about 110 °F (43 ° C.) in the jars at normal temperature for approximately 20 minutes, but keep it above 100 degrees F. (37 degrees C). A greater temperature will destroy the probiotic bacteria; therefore, this is crucial.
- Over each container, crack open or cut 1 probiotic capsule, then whisk in the powder. Put lids on top.
- Turn on your oven's light to start a yogurt incubation (not the oven). Based on how tangy you need your yogurt to be, lay the jars onto a sheet pan & bake for 12 to 24 hours with the door closed & the light on. (As an alternative, you may keep the jars warm by wrapping a blanket over them.
- After the yogurt is finished, chill it in the refrigerator. Stir well since it will be thick. Enjoy with Hemp Hearts on top!

Nutritional values per serving:
Total Calories: 236kcal, **Fat:** 24g, **Carbohydrates:** 2g, **Protein:** 3g

27. Oatmeal

Ready in: 10 mins.
Serves: 1
Difficulty: easy
Ingredients:

- 1 tbsp. of flax seed meal
- 1/4 cup of Hemp seeds (hulled)
- 1 tbsp. of Collagen protein powder
- 1/2 cup of Coconut milk
- 1/2 tbsp. of Chia seeds

Optional add-ins:

- 1 pinch of Sea salt
- 1 tbsp. of Fruit Allulose Blend (Besti Monk)

Directions:

- In a small saucepan, combine all the ingredients, aside from cream or milk, while stirring.
- Whisk in the cream or milk until smooth.

Nutritional values per serving:
Total Calories: 596kcal, **Fat:** 48g, **Carbohydrates:** 10g, **Protein:** 28g

28. Coffee

Ready in: 5 mins.
Serves: 1
Difficulty: easy
Ingredients:

- 1 tbsp. of butter, unsalted (can also use coconut oil or ghee)
- 8 fl. Oz. of brewed Coffee
- 1 tsp. of MCT Oil

Optional add-ins:

- 1 tbsp. of Collagen protein powder
- 1/2 cup of almond milk, unsweetened (vanilla or regular)
- 1 tbsp. of Coffee Syrup (or some more to taste)

Directions:

- In a blender, combine all the ingredients. 5 to 15 seconds, or until frothy and creamy, in a blender. (Alternatively, emulsify the mixture using a milk frother in your cup or a tall container, but be very sure to allow space for it to spread.)
- To serve, pour into the coffee cup.

Nutritional values per serving:
Total Calories: 180kcal, **Fat:** 16g, **Carbohydrates:** 0g, **Protein:** 0g

29. Protein Shake

Ready in: 5 mins.
Serves: 6
Difficulty: easy
Ingredients:

- 2 cups of Raspberries
- 2 cups of Strawberries (hulled)
- 1 1/2 cups of Blueberries
- 1 can of coconut milk, full-fat (14.5 oz.), including cream & liquid
- 3/4 cup of Collagen protein powder
- 3/4 cup of Simple Syrup or to taste
- 1 tbsp. of Lemon juice
- 6 tbsp. of MCT oil powder

Directions:

- Blend each item in a blender until completely smooth.
- To taste, adjust the sweetener for simple syrup as necessary.

Nutritional values per serving:
Total Calories: 131kcal, **Fat:** 3g, **Carbohydrates:** 15g, **Protein:** 12g

30. Peanut Butter Chocolate Smoothie

Ready in: 5 mins.
Serves: 3
Difficulty: easy
Ingredients:

- 3 tbsp. of Cocoa powder
- 1/4 cup of creamy Peanut butter
- 1 cup of Heavy cream
- 6 tbsp. of Besti Powdered Erythritol
- 1 1/2 cups of almond milk, unsweetened (vanilla or regular)
- 1/8 tsp. of Sea salt (it's optional)

Directions:

- In a blender, combine all the ingredients.
- Blend until smooth. When needed, taste-test the sweetener.

Nutritional values per serving:
Total Calories: 435kcal, **Fat:** 41g, **Carbohydrates:** 10g, **Protein:** 9g

CHAPTER 3:
Keto Diet - Lunch Recipes Vegan/Vegetarian Recipes

1. Portobello Mushroom Burger

Ready in: 45 mins.
Serves: 2
Difficulty: easy
Ingredients:

- 120 g of plain tofu
- 4 Portobello mushrooms
- 1/2 tomato (medium-sized)
- 3 tsp. of mustard, sugar-free
- 2 salad leaves (large)
- 2 1/2 tbsp. of olive oil
- Some black pepper
- 2 tbsp. of tamari (or you can also use soy sauce)
- Some ground cumin (optional)

Directions:

- Clean Portobello mushrooms are combined with 1 tablespoon tamari, 1 1/2 tablespoons olive oil, a dash of ground cumin, and 1/8 teaspoon of black pepper. Use your hands to combine the ingredients, but watch out for the mushrooms since they may break easily. The mushrooms may either be cooked right away or chilled for around 15 minutes.
- Cut the tofu into 2-4 pieces that are thick. Use one tbsp of olive oil rather than two and a half to make the same marinade for tofu. You have the option of cooking it right away or giving it about 20 minutes to sit in the refrigerator.
- The remaining veggies needed for the dish should be washed and chopped to your taste.
- Bake the mushrooms in a 180°C preheated oven for 10 to 15 minutes. To prevent them from becoming too dry, turn them a few times. During the last five minutes of cooking, leave the oven door open to keep the cooked mushrooms tender but not watery.
- You may bake the mushrooms and tofu together. Cook it for 8 to 10 mins to keep your tofu soft or till golden for a crunchy outcome, depending on your tastes.
- When the tofu and mushrooms are just beginning to warm up, assemble the patties and serve right away. While you may prepare the ingredi-

ents ahead of time, it's best to assemble the burgers right before serving.

Nutritional values per serving:
Total Calories: 253kcal, **Fat:** 20g, **Carbohydrates:** 10g, **Protein:** 10g

2. Zucchini Pizza

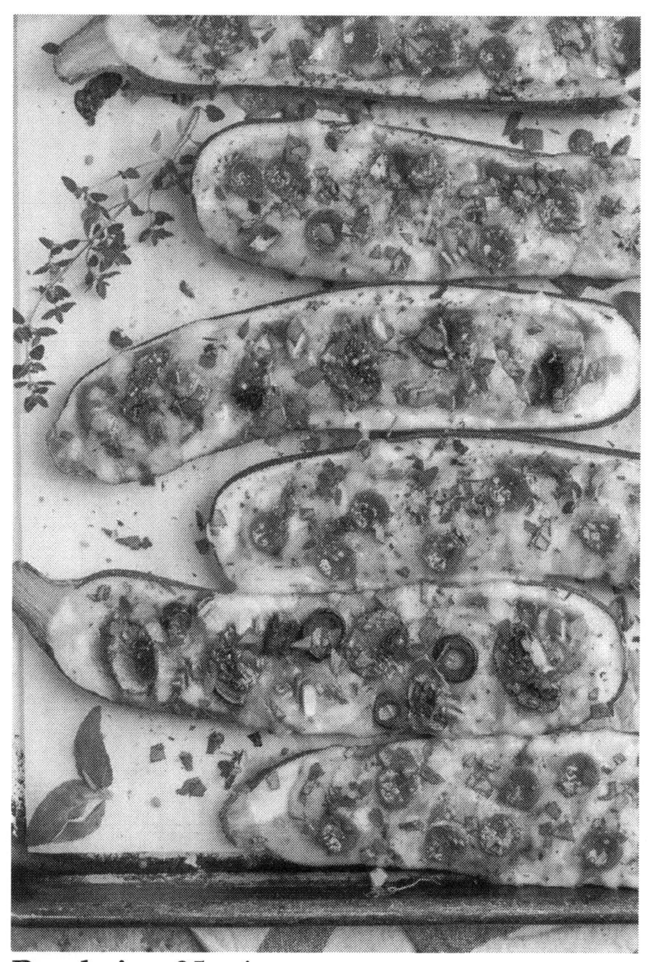

Ready in: 35 mins.
Serves: 6
Difficulty: easy
Ingredients:

- 2 tsp. of Psyllium husk powder
- 3/4 cup of sunflower seeds (100 g)
- 1 zucchini (230 g)
- ½ to 3/4 tsp. of salt
- 1 tsp. of Italian seasoning (optional)
- 1 tbsp. of nutritional yeast

Directions:

- Grate the zucchini, then press out any extra juice
- Also, preheat your oven to 360° F (180 degrees C) & cover a baking sheet using parchment paper that has been greased.
- Sunflower seeds should be ground with Psyllium husk powder, nutritional yeast, salt, and Italian spice. To blend, stir.
- Use a spoon to stir everything together after adding this mixture into the zucchini. The dough should then be thoroughly combined using your hands.
- Use your fingers to spread the dough on the prepared baking sheet, then bake it for approximately 15 minutes till the edges begin to become golden brown.
- Prepare your preferred toppings in the meanwhile.
- Pizza with a topping should bake for an additional 10-15 minutes. Enjoy!
- The pizza would be ready much quicker if you add a few toppings, such as vegan cheese & olives (for instance), rather than many different vegetables.

Nutritional values per serving:
Total Calories: 110kcal, **Fat:** 8g, **Carbohydrates:** 2g, **Protein:** 4g

3. Collard Green Wraps

Ready in: 15 mins.
Serves: 4

Difficulty: easy

Ingredients:

- 1/2 cup of Cauliflower hummus
- 4 Collard leaves, large (washed & dried)
- 3 oz. of Cucumber (in short, thin strips)
- 1 Roma tomato, medium (diced)
- 1/2 Bell pepper, large (cut in short, thin strips)
- 1 Avocado, medium (sliced)
- 1/4 cup of Red onion (in thin half-moons)

Directions:

- Trim the collard green stems' thickest portion using a paring knife.
- Spread two tbsp. (30 grams) of cauliflower hummus over each collard leaf, leaving a 1-inch (2.5-centimeter) border without it to prevent seepage. Add cucumbers, red onions, bell peppers, and tomatoes, then, in that order, avocado on the top. All the vegetables should be arranged lengthwise in a single direction that is perpendicular to the leaf's length.
- Start wrapping the wraps from the broad side. The ends should be folded in first, then rolled up just like a burrito. (You should roll parallel to how the vegetables are sliced and arranged.)
- Put seam side down & repeat with the rest of the collard wraps.

Nutritional values per serving:

Total Calories: 208kcal, **Fat:** 17g, **Carbohydrates:** 12g, **Protein:** 4g

4. Almond Butter Lettuce Wraps

Ready in: 30 mins.

Serves: 4

Difficulty: easy

Ingredients:

- 15 oz. of tofu (extra firm), drained
- 2 tbsp. of sesame oil
- 1 diced onion
- 1 tbsp. of rice vinegar
- 3 tbsp. of tamari
- 2 cloves of garlic, minced
- ¼ cup of red cabbage, chopped
- 2 tbsp. of water chestnuts
- ¼ cup of chopped red peppers
- 1 head of butter lettuce
- 2 tbsp. of chopped almonds

For almond butter sauce:

- 1 tbsp. of tamari
- 2 tbsp. of almond butter
- 1 tsp. of garlic powder
- 1 tsp. of rice vinegar
- 1 tsp. of ground ginger

Directions:

- In a skillet on medium-high heat, warm the sesame oil. Add the tofu, broken up into pieces, to the skillet. Continue chopping the tofu into a grainy mixture using a spatula. For around 10 minutes, brown the tofu.
- Using a spatula break the tofu into tiny pieces in a pan.
- Add tamari, onion, and rice wine vinegar after stirring. Sauté for approximately 5 minutes or until onions are soft. Garlic, red pepper, water chestnuts, cabbage, & almonds are all stirred in. Sauté the peppers

for some more minutes or until they are barely soft.

- With a spatula and stir a pan with tofu filled with vegetables.
- Combine the ingredients and whisk them to make the almond butter sauce. Stirring to ensure that all of the tofu mixtures are covered, add half the sauce to the pan.
- Place one or two spoonfuls of the veggie-tofu mixture in the middle of each lettuce leaf before serving. Serve with the sauce of your choice or the saved almond butter sauce.

Nutritional values per serving:
Total Calories: 238kcal, **Fat:** 16g, **Carbohydrates:** 11g, **Protein:** 13g

5. No Bean Chili

Ready in: 40 mins.
Serves: 7
Difficulty: easy
Ingredients:

- 5 stalks of finely diced celery
- 2 tbsp. of olive Oil
- 2 cloves of garlic, minced
- 2 tsp. of chili powder
- 1 1/2 tsp. of ground cinnamon
- 4 tsp. of ground cumin
- 2 chipotle peppers in adobo, large (minced)
- 1 ½ tsp. of smoked paprika
- 2 finely diced green bell peppers
- 8 oz. of minced cremini mushrooms
- 2 diced zucchini
- 1 1/2 tbsp. of tomato paste
- 3 cups of water
- 1 can of diced tomatoes (15 oz.)
- 1/2 cup of coconut milk
- 1 cup of walnuts (raw), minced
- 2 1/2 cups of soy meat crumbled
- Salt & pepper to taste
- 1 tbsp. of cocoa powder, unsweetened

To serve:

- 1 sliced Avocado
- 2 tbsp. of cilantro leaves, fresh
- 2 tbsp. of sliced radishes

Directions:

- In a big saucepan, warm the oil over medium heat. Cook the celery for 4 minutes after adding it. Stir for a further two minutes or until the garlic, chili powder, cinnamon, cumin, and paprika are aromatic.

- Cook for 4-5 minutes after adding the zucchini, bell peppers, and mushrooms.
- Put the water, soy meat, coconut milk, walnuts, cocoa powder, tomato paste, chipotle, and tomato paste into a saucepan. Once thick and the veggies are tender, lower the heat to medium and let the mixture simmer for approximately 20 to 25 minutes.
- To taste, add salt and pepper to the dish. Add radishes, avocado, & cilantro as garnish.

Nutritional values per serving:
Total Calories: 353kcal, **Fat:** 28g, **Carbohydrates:** 18g, **Protein:** 13g

6. Lemon Pesto Zoodles

Ready in: 30 mins.
Serves: 4
Difficulty: easy
Ingredients:
For Lemon Pesto:

- 1/2 cup of parsley packed, fresh
- 1.5 cups of basil leaves packed, fresh
- 1/3 cup of pine nuts
- 2 cloves of garlic peeled
- 1/2 cup of nutritional yeast
- 1/2 tsp. of salt
- 1 tbsp. of lemon juice
- 1/4 tsp. of black pepper
- 1/2 cup of olive oil
- 1.5 tbsp. of lemon zest

For Zoodles:

- 1 pound bunch of asparagus
- 6-8 zucchini (medium)
- 1 tbsp. of olive oil

Directions:
Making pesto:

- In a food processor, combine walnuts, parsley, and basil. Once roughly chopped, pulse (about 8 times).
- Lemon juice, lemon zest, nutritional yeast, salt, and pepper should all be added. Mix on low.
- Slowly add olive oil into the food processor while it is running to emulsify till well combined. If necessary, taste and adjust the salt and pepper.

Make zoodles:

- Zoodles are spiralized, then put aside.
- Asparagus should have its rough ends removed and sliced into 1-inch sections.
- Over medium heat, warm 1 tablespoon of olive oil in a pan. Add the asparagus and cook it until it is bright green and fork-tender (5-7 minutes).
- Zoodles and pesto should be mixed well before adding. Cook for 1-2 minutes or until well heated.
- Heat through and serve warm. Overages last for around 5 days.

Nutritional values per serving:
Total Calories: 442kcal, **Fat:** 34g, **Carbohydrates:** 26g, **Protein:** 17g

7. Cauliflower Rice, Mushrooms Risotto

Ready in: 20 mins.
Serves: 6
Difficulty: easy

Ingredients:

- 2 cloves of finely chopped garlic or minced
- 2 tbsp. of coconut oil (butter flavored)
- 1 head of cauliflower
- ½ cup of coconut cream
- 3.4 ounces of mushrooms, chopped
- Fresh parsley to garnish
- 1 tbsp. of nutritional yeast

Directions:

- Coconut oil should be melted in a big pan over medium-high heat. When the garlic is aromatic and beginning to turn golden, add it.
- Add the mushrooms and cook for approximately 4 minutes or until they are soft and gently browned.
- After the mushrooms and riced cauliflower are properly combined, add them together.
- Coconut cream & nutritional yeast are cooked by being combined. Serve after removing from heat and adding a parsley garnish.

Nutritional values per serving:
Total Calories: 139kcal, **Fat:** 11g, **Carbohydrates:** 7g, **Protein:** 3g

8. Mushrooms Steaks

Ready in: 15 mins.
Serves: 4
Difficulty: easy
Ingredients:

- 2-3 tbsp. of olive oil
- 4 Portobello mushrooms (large)
- 2 tsp. of tamari soy sauce
- salt to taste
- 1 tsp. of garlic purée

Directions:

- Set the air fryer's temperature to 350°F/180°C.
- Remove the stems from the mushrooms and clean them with a moist brush or towel.
- Olive oil, garlic purée, tamari soy sauce, and salt are combined in a bowl.
- When the mushrooms are evenly coated, add them in. The mixture may also be applied to the mushrooms using a brush. The mushrooms may either be cooked right away or rested for 10 mins before cooking.
- In the air fryer basket, add the mushrooms and cook for 8 to 10 minutes.
- Serve some salad leaves beside the garlicky air-fried mushrooms.

Nutritional values per serving:
Total Calories: 84kcal, **Fat:** 7g, **Carbohydrates:** 4g, **Protein:** 2g

9. Sunflower Seed Cheese Courgetti

Ready in: 20 mins.
Serves: 2
Difficulty: easy
Ingredients:

- 3 Zucchini/Courgette
- 1 cup of Sunflower seeds
- 3 tbsp. of Nutritional yeast
- 3 tbsp. of Sesame seeds
- 1 clove of garlic
- ¼ tsp. of Turmeric
- 2 tsp. of Salt

- 1 tbsp. of Apple cider vinegar
- Water for blending and soaking
- 12 Basil leaves
- 6 Cherry tomatoes

Directions:

- Sunflower seeds should be soaked in a little salt for one hour or even overnight.
- Sunflower seeds should be drained before being combined with nutritional yeast, sesame, garlic, vinegar, and turmeric in a blender.
- Only enough water will be needed to make a smooth paste in your blender.
- Use a spiralizer to create thin strips from your courgette or zucchini, or if you don't have one, use a vegetable peeler or julienne slicer.
- A sprinkle of salt should be massaged into the courgette spaghetti until the volume is reduced by roughly a third and the juices are released.
- Cheese made from sunflower seeds should be included now.
- Any leftover zucchini noodles should be refrigerated and used within 48 hours.

Nutritional values per serving:
Total Calories: 286kcal, **Fat:** 22g, **Carbohydrates:** 17g, **Protein:** 13g

10. Street Tacos

Ready in: 40 mins.
Serves: 5
Difficulty: easy
Ingredients:

- 2 cups of raw walnuts (250g)
- 3 cups of cauliflower florets

For Seasoning:

- 1 tsp. of onion powder
- 1 tsp. of garlic powder
- 1 tbsp. of chili powder
- 1 1/2 tsp. of dried oregano
- 2 tsp. of cumin
- Some sea salt and pepper
- 1 tbsp. of hot sauce

For Garnish:

- Some fresh lime juice

Directions:

- Heat the oven to 375F.
- All ingredients, excluding the garnish, should be placed in a food processor. Blend in short bursts until fully combined and paste-like. Spread out the "meat" mixture before adding it to a baking sheet covered with parchment paper. About halfway through the cooking process, turn the mixture over and cut it up. Bake for approximately 35 minutes or until the sides are toasted and golden.
- After done, allow the meat to cool somewhat before serving!

Nutritional values per serving:
Total Calories: 397kcal, **Fat:** 33g, **Carbohydrates:** 18g, **Protein:** 12g

11. Creamy Brussels Sprout Spaghetti

Ready in: 25 mins.
Serves: 1
Difficulty: easy
Ingredients:

- 1/4 cup of Brussels sprouts, shredded

- 1 package of shirataki noodles
- 1 clove of garlic
- 1 tbsp. of olive oil
- 2 tbsp. of vegan cream cheese
- salt & pepper to taste
- 1 tbsp. of nutritional yeast

Directions:

- Brussels sprouts, garlic, and olive oil should all be added to the pan & sautéed for a few mins till the garlic and sprouts start to soften.
- The noodles should be rinsed and drained before being added to the pan, along with the other ingredients.
- Once the ingredients are fully combined to form a creamy sauce, whisk about once per minute.
- When the sauce reaches the desired alfredo-like consistency, add a small bit (up to a tbsp.) of water and whisk.
- Plate the spaghetti and eat it when Brussels sprouts are tender, and the sauce is hot.

Nutritional values per serving:
Total Calories: 259kcal, **Fat:** 23g, **Carbohydrates:** 9g, **Protein:** 7g

12. Romesco Cabbage Noodles

Ready in: 30 mins.
Serves: 4
Difficulty: easy
Ingredients:
For noodles:

- ½ tbsp. of avocado oil
- 1 head of green cabbage
- ¼ tsp. of fine salt

For Sauce:

- ¼ cup of avocado oil
- ¼ cup of shelled hemp seeds
- ½ Vidalia onion (small), sliced.
- 1 tsp. of garlic powder or 1 to 2 garlic cloves (large), smashed
- ½ tsp. of salt
- 2 tbsp. of green olives, chopped

Directions:

- Set the oven to 400 °F.
- Core and cut your cabbage in half. Put one-half of the cabbage's flat side down & start slicing it from the round side. The cabbage should be cut into confetti-like pieces. The size of cabbage will affect the yield.
- No more than five cups of shreds of cabbage should be placed on each sheet pan when using the oil & salt recommendations above. Toss your cabbage with salt and oil.
- Roast for 10 to 15 minutes or until fork-tender and gently browned.
- Heat a small pan over high heat to begin preparing the sauce. Heat while adding the seeds until just browned. Take out of the skillet.
- Onions and oil should be added. Sauté the onions in hot oil until golden.
- In a food processor or blender, combine the toasted seeds, fried onions, and the other ingredients. Process until a thick sauce is formed. Eat the noodles after spooning the sauce over them.

Nutritional values per serving:
Total Calories: 244kcal, **Fat:** 22g, **Carbohydrates:** 7g, **Protein:** 4g

13. Shepherd's Pie

Ready in: 1 hr.
Serves: 6
Difficulty: easy
Ingredients:
For Topping:

- ½ tsp. of garlic powder
- 1 cauliflower (medium)
- 1 tsp. of salt
- 1 tbsp. of nutritional yeast
- ½ tsp. of black pepper

For Filling:

- 2 cloves of garlic, chopped
- 1 onion (medium), chopped
- 1 cup of hemp hearts
- 5 stalks of celery chopped
- 1 tbsp. of tomato paste
- 2 cups of mushrooms, chopped
- 1 tbsp. of thyme
- 1 cup of walnuts chopped
- 1 tsp. of Dijon mustard
- 1 cup of vegetable stock
- 3 tbsp. of olive oil

Directions:

Making the topping:

- Cut the cauliflower into florets after trimming. Put the ingredients in a medium pot with water, and then heat to a boil. The cauliflower should be tender after 10 to 15 minutes of simmering undercover.
- Drain the water after removing the cauliflower from the heat.
- Use a fork or a potato ricer to mash the cauliflower.
- Mix thoroughly after adding the spice and nutritional year.

Creating the filling:

- In a big frying pan over medium heat, warm the olive oil. For three minutes, add the garlic and onion and simmer until tender.
- Cook for another 5-7 minutes, stirring regularly to achieve uniform cooking, after adding the mushrooms and celery.
- Cook for a further five minutes after adding the tomato paste, mustard, and stock.
- Add the spice, hemp hearts, and chopped walnuts. Cook for 5 mins while stirring well. Taste the spice and tweak it to suit your tastes.

Assemble:

- Set the oven's temperature to 190 C/375 F.
- Large ramekin dishes or 1 baking dish should be filled with the contents.
- The mashed cauliflower should be piped or spooned over the contents.
- For 20 to 30 minutes, bake.

Nutritional values per serving:
Total Calories: 434kcal, **Fat:** 35g, **Carbohydrates:** 15g, **Protein:** 19g

14. Peanut Butter Tofu & Sriracha

Ready in: 40 mins.
Serves: 4
Difficulty: easy
Ingredients:

- 1 tbsp. of peanut oil
- 16 oz. of firm tofu
- Some garlic cloves (large), sliced
- 2 tbsp. of green onions, diagonally sliced (for garnish)
- one piece of ginger root (large), sliced

For sauce:

- 3 tbsp. of rice vinegar
- 3 tbsp. of soy sauce
- 2 tbsp. of smooth peanut butter (natural)
- 2 tbsp. of water or vegetable stock
- 1 tbsp. of Monkfruit sweetener
- 1 tbsp. of Sriracha Sauce

Directions:

- With a colander positioned in the sink, thoroughly drain the tofu.
- In order for the tofu's liquid to be absorbed by the towel, place the tofu pieces between two layers of paper towels & push down with your palm. (If necessary, repeat this multiple times.)
- Tofu should be cut into 1-inch-wide strips lengthwise.
- Add Sriracha Sauce after whisking the soy sauce, peanut butter, rice vinegar, monk fruit sweetener, and water or vegetable stock together
- Green onions should be sliced diagonally, along with the pieces of ginger and garlic.
- The dry wok should be heated for one minute on high.
- Then add your peanut oil and cook for 30 seconds longer.
- Next, remove and discard the ginger and garlic slices after cooking them for about 30 seconds or so or until they are aromatic.
- Add the tofu pieces, reduce the heat to medium-high, and cook, stirring often, for approximately 7-8 minutes or until the tofu is evenly browned on both sides.
- After all of the tofu is browned, add your sauce, reduce heat, and simmer just long enough for the sauce to coat the tofu and slightly thicken. (Don't simmer for too long; if you do, the sauce will thicken and become too thick to pour over the pieces of tofu)

- Take the pan off the heat.
- Transfer the tofu pieces to a dish and pour sauce all over and garnish with some green onion slices.
- Serve warm.

Nutritional values per serving:
Total Calories: 191kcal, **Fat:** 14g, **Carbohydrates:** 6g, **Protein:** 15g

15. Cauliflower Mushroom Rice with Peppers

Ready in: 20 mins.
Serves: 4
Difficulty: easy
Ingredients:

- 8 oz. of mushrooms
- 1 lb. of cauliflower rice
- 1 bell pepper
- ⅓ cup of olive oil
- 1 cup of chopped onions
- 1 tsp. of bouillon powder
- 1 tsp. of black pepper
- ½ tsp. of cayenne pepper
- ½ tsp. of thyme
- Scallions, for garnishing
- ½ tsp. of salt

Directions:

- Mushrooms should be washed and drained.
- When the olive oil in a pan is hot, add the chopped onions.
- Stir the bell peppers & mushrooms in, after adding them after the onions start to turn brown.
- Salt, cayenne pepper, thyme, black pepper, and bouillon powder should also be added.
- Mix everything together, then simmer for approximately five minutes while stirring occasionally.
- Throw the cauliflower rice in and toss until everything is well combined.
- Add salt as needed after tasting.
- Simmer for around 5 minutes or until the texture is to your liking.
- Enjoy after garnishing with scallions!

Nutritional values per serving:
Total Calories: 217kcal, **Fat:** 18g, **Carbohydrates:** 9g, **Protein:** 5g

16. Broccoli Stir-Fry with Garlic Sauce

Ready in: 20 mins.
Serves: 6

Difficulty: easy
Ingredients:

- 2 tbsp. of avocado oil
- 3 to 4 lbs. of Chinese broccoli, about 6 to 8 tightly packed cups
- 2 tsp. of garlic cloves, grated
- 1-2 tsp. of sesame oil (toasted), garnish
- 1/2 tsp. of sea salt, divided
- 1 tbsp. of coconut aminos, garnish

Directions:

- Stems of Chinese broccoli bottom should have the lowest inch or so removed and thrown away. Make another incision to remove stems from leafy portions. Cut the stems at a diagonal angle to a length of about 2 to 2-12 inches. Trim the leafy portions in half. Stems and leafy portions should be washed and rinsed separately. Put them aside in separate bowls to drain.
- Add 2 tbsp. Frying oil to a big skillet (or wok) that has been preheated. Place the stems in a pot and cook them over medium-high until they become brilliant green (about 2 minutes). Sprinkle on 1/4 teaspoon of coarse salt. With a wooden spoon , smash and distribute the grated garlic over the veggies after adding it.
- Add leafy components. The stems & garlic should be tossed and scooped over the leaves quickly. Place a lid on top. Heat is reduced to medium. The leaves should be cooked for 3 minutes or until they are a dark green color. Sprinkle on 1/4 teaspoon of coarse salt. Give a fast throw. Dispose of heat and transfer to a big platter.
- Add coconut aminos and toasted sesame oil for seasoning.

Nutritional values per serving:
Total Calories: 86kcal, **Fat:** 7g, **Carbohydrates:** 4g, **Protein:** 1g

17. Three Cheese Stuffed Peppers Quiche

Ready in: 1 hr.
Serves: 4
Difficulty: easy
Ingredients:

- 4 eggs (large)
- 2 bell peppers (medium), sliced in half & seeds removed
- ½ cup of ricotta cheese
- ½ cup of Parmesan cheese (grated)
- ½ cup of shredded mozzarella
- 1 tsp. of garlic powder
- ¼ cup of baby spinach leaves
- ¼ tsp. of dried parsley
- 2 tbsp. of Parmesan cheese for garnishing

Directions:

- The oven should be heated to 375 degrees Fahrenheit. Remove the seeds from the peppers and cut them into 4-5 equal pieces.
- Combine the eggs, three slices of cheese, garlic powder, parsley, and a small food processor.
- Each pepper should be filled with the egg mixture to just below the rim. Using a fork, swirl the surface to tuck a few young spinach leaves below the egg. Bake for 35 to 45

minutes, till the egg, is set, covered with foil.

- When the tops start to brown, garnish with Parmesan cheese & broil for 3 to 5 minutes.

Nutritional values per serving:
Total Calories: 245.5kcal, **Fat:** 16.28g, **Carbohydrates:** 5.97g, **Protein:** 17.84g

18. Sesame Tofu & Eggplant

Ready in: 1 hr.
Serves: 4
Difficulty: easy
Ingredients:

- 1 cup of chopped cilantro (31g)
- 1 pound of block firm tofu
- 3 tbsp. of rice vinegar
- 2 finely minced cloves of garlic
- 4 tbsp. of toasted sesame oil
- 1 tsp. of red pepper flakes, crushed
- 1 whole eggplant (458 g)
- 2 tsp. of sugar
- 1 tbsp. of olive oil
- ¼ cup of sesame seeds
- Salt & pepper to taste
- ¼ cup of soy sauce

Directions:

- Set the oven to 200 °F. Take the tofu block out of its container, then wrap it in some paper towels. Put a plate above it to act as a weight. In this photograph, I used a rather big can of veggies, but you may use whatever you have on hand. For a time, let the tofu rest to squeeze some of the water out.
- A big mixing bowl should include around 1/4 cup cilantro, 3 tbsp. of rice vinegar, 2 teaspoons toasted sesame oil, chopped garlic, red pepper flakes, & Sugar. Blend well.
- The eggplant should be peeled and julienned. Combine the marinade and the eggplant.
- Over low heat, add the tbsp of olive oil to the skillet. Eggplant should be cooked until it softens. If the eggplant is clinging to the pan, add a little extra sesame or olive oil; the eggplant will absorb all of the juices. Just be careful to change how you monitor your nutrition.
- Switch off the oven. Transfer the noodles to a dish that can go in the oven after stirring the leftover cilantro into the eggplant. Place the dish in the oven to maintain warmth and cover using a lid or foil. Clean the skillet, then put it back on the burner to reheat.
- Tofu should be unwrapped and sliced into 8 pieces. On a dish, scatter the sesame seeds. Each tofu piece should be pressed into the seeds from both sides.
- To the skillet, add 2 teaspoons of sesame oil. Fried the tofu for five minutes on each side or until it begins to crisp up. Coat the tofu chunks with the 1/4 cup soy sauce that has been added to the pan. Using the soy sauce, cook the tofu pieces until they appear browned and caramelized.
- Place the tofu above the noodles after taking them out of the oven.

Nutritional values per serving:
Total Calories: 292.75kcal, **Fat:** 25g, **Carbohydrates:** 7g, **Protein:** 11.21g

19. Fried Mac and Cheese

Ready in: 30 mins.
Serves: 27
Difficulty: easy
Ingredients:

- 1 ½ cups of cheddar cheese, shredded
- 1 cauliflower (medium), riced
- 3 eggs (large)
- 1 tsp. of turmeric
- 2 tsp. of paprika
- ¾ tsp. of rosemary

Directions:

- In a food processor, rice the cauliflower.
- It needs five minutes in the microwave to cook.
- Wring it out in a kitchen towel or some paper towels to dry it. The least amount of wetness is ideal.
- Cauliflower should be combined with the eggs (1 at a time since you do not want a watery combination), cheese, and seasonings.
- In a pan, heat the coconut oil and olive oil on high.
- From the cauliflower mixture, make little patties.
- Fry till crisp on both sides.

Nutritional values per serving:
Total Calories: 39.67kcal, **Fat:** 2.71g, **Carbohydrates:** 0.96g, **Protein:** 2.59g

20. Red Coconut Curry

Ready in: 30 mins.
Serves: 2
Difficulty: easy
Ingredients:

- 1 handful of spinach (large)
- 1 cup of broccoli florets
- 4 tbsp. of coconut oil
- 1 tsp. of minced garlic
- ¼ onion (medium)
- 1 tsp. of minced ginger
- 2 tsp. of soy sauce
- 2 tsp. of Fish sauce
- ½ cup of coconut cream or milk
- 1 tbsp. of red curry paste

Directions:

- Cut up some minced garlic and onions. In a pan, add 2 tbsp of coconut oil and heat over medium-high.
- When the pan is heated, add the onions and sauté them until they are transparent. Add garlic into the pan after that to brown it.
- Reduce heat to medium-low, then stir in broccoli. Mix everything well.
- Broccoli should be halfway cooked before adding curry paste and moving veggies to one side of the pan. Cook for 45 to 60 seconds.
- Add the spinach above the broccoli starts to wilt, put the remaining coconut oil & cream of coconut.
- Soy sauce, fish sauce, and ginger are combined and stirred together. Depending on the desired thickness, let simmer for 5 to 10 minutes.

Nutritional values per serving:
Total Calories: 398kcal, **Fat:** 40.73g, **Carbohydrates:** 7.86g, **Protein:** 3.91g

POULTRY RECIPES

1. Cauliflower Mac and Cheese

Ready in: 30 mins.
Serves: 8
Difficulty: easy
Ingredients:

- 1 cup of heavy whipping cream
- 2 pounds of cauliflower florets, frozen
- 4 ounces of cream cheese, cubed
- 1 tsp. of Dijon mustard
- 8 ounces of shredded cheddar cheese
- 1 tsp. of turmeric
- Salt & pepper to taste
- ½ tsp. of powdered garlic

Directions:

- Cook the florets of cauliflower as per the package directions.
- The cream should simmer. Add the cream cheese & blend with a whisk until smooth.
- 6 ounces of shredded cheddar cheese should be added. Save the remaining 2 ounces for a later time. Stir the cheese into the sauce until it melts.
- Salt, pepper, turmeric, Dijon mustard, and garlic powder should all be added. The sauce would become a uniform shade of yellow.
- Make sure the cauliflower has been well drained before adding it to the cheese sauce. Apply sauce evenly to the florets.
- The last 2 oz. of cheddar cheese should be sprinkled over and stirred until mostly melted.

Nutritional values per serving:
Total Calories: 295.5kcal, **Fat:** 25.38g, **Carbohydrates:** 5.47g, **Protein:** 10.63g

2. Tomato Basil & Mozzarella Galette

Ready in: 1 hr.
Serves: 3
Difficulty: easy
Ingredients:

- 1 egg (large)
- 1 cup of almond flour
- 3 tbsp. of mozzarella liquid
- ¼ cup of Parmesan cheese, shredded
- 1 tsp. of garlic powder

- 2 tbsp. of pesto
- ½ ounce of Mozzarella
- 3-4 leaves of fresh basil
- 3 cherry tomatoes

Directions:

- Place parchment on a cookie sheet and preheat the oven to 375°F. Use nonstick spray to coat. Gently whisk the mozzarella liquid, almond flour, and garlic powder together in a bowl.
- As dough forms, thoroughly combine the egg & Parmesan cheese.
- Create a huge ball out of the dough mixture, and then set it on the prepared paper.
- While attempting to maintain a consistent thickness, press the ball of dough into a circular. The thickness should be roughly half an inch. While it could be sticky, a little water on your hands will help prevent your fingers from collecting up the crust.
- Distribute the pesto over the crust's center evenly, allowing space around the sides to fold it in. tomatoes, basil leaves, and mozzarella are layered.
- Fold the crust's edges up & over the filling using the side of the parchment paper. Up until all the sides are folded, move in a round around the edge.
- Once cheese is melted, and crust is browned, bake for 20-25 minutes.

Nutritional values per serving:
Total Calories: 971kcal, **Fat:** 72g, **Carbohydrates:** 33g, **Protein:** 43g

3. Tuscan Creamy Garlic Chicken

Ready in: 25 mins.
Serves: 6
Difficulty: easy
Ingredients:

- 2 tbsp. of olive oil
- 1½ pounds of skinless, boneless, thinly sliced chicken breasts
- 1 cup of heavy cream
- 1 tsp. of garlic powder
- 1/2 cup of chicken broth
- 1 tsp. of Italian seasoning
- 1 cup of chopped spinach
- 1/2 cup of parmesan cheese
- 1/2 cup of sun-dried tomatoes

Directions:

- Olive oil should be added to a big pan, and the chicken should be cooked for three to five mins per side or till it is brown and not pink in the middle. Take the chicken out and place it on a platter.

- Add the parmesan cheese, heavy cream, chicken stock, garlic powder, and Italian seasoning. Stir until the mixture begins to thicken over medium-high heat. Sundried tomatoes and spinach should be added, and the mixture should boil until the spinach begins to wilt. If preferred, serve the chicken over spaghetti after adding it back to the pan.

Nutritional values per serving:
Total Calories: 368kcal, **Fat:** 25g, **Carbohydrates:** 7g, **Protein:** 30g

4. Spinach & Goat Cheese Stuffed Chicken Breast with Mushrooms & Caramelized Onions

Ready in: 45 mins.
Serves: 4
Difficulty: easy
Ingredients:

- 2 tbsp. of olive oil, divided
- 4 (4-6 ounces each) chicken breasts
- 4 cups of organic spinach
- 2 ounces of goat cheese
- ½ tsp. of garlic powder
- 1 sliced white onion
- 1 tsp. of fresh thyme
- 8 ounces of baby bella mushrooms, sliced
- Freshly ground salt & pepper
- Optional: 1 tbsp. of balsamic vinegar

Directions:

- Set oven up to 375 degrees Fahrenheit. Each chicken breast should have six slits cut into the top of it using a sharp knife. Sprinkle salt and pepper over each chicken breast after drizzling it with some olive oil. Set aside.
- 1/2 tbsp. of olive oil is added to a large ovenproof pan, and it is heated to medium-high. Garlic powder should be added together with the spinach. Sauté the spinach until it has completely wilted, stirring periodically.
- Goat cheese and cooked spinach should be combined in a medium bowl. Stir well to mix. Insert the spinach & goat cheese mixture into each incision.

- The same skillet should now have 1 tbsp of olive oil added. Sliced onions, fresh thyme, mushrooms, optional balsamic vinegar, and a touch of salt and pepper may all be added. Sauté until mushrooms become golden brown, and onions start to caramelize. Move the onions and mushrooms to the edges of the pan to make space for the chicken.
- Place the chicken in the pan, leaving some space between each of the chicken breasts; you might have to reposition the mushrooms & onions. Move the chicken to the oven, and bake for 30 minutes or until the internal temperature of the chicken reaches 165 degrees F.

Nutritional values per serving:
Total Calories: 239kcal, **Fat:** 12g, **Carbohydrates:** 5g, **Protein:** 28g

5. Chicken Enchilada Bowl

Ready in: 50 mins.
Serves: 4
Difficulty: easy
Ingredients:

- 1 pound of skinless, boneless chicken thighs
- 2 tbsp. of coconut oil
- ¾ cup of red enchilada sauce
- ¼ cup of chopped onion
- ¼ cup of water
- 4 oz. can of diced green chiles

Toppings:

- 1 cup of cheese, shredded
- 1 avocado (whole), diced
- ¼ cup of pickled jalapenos, chopped
- 1 chopped Roma tomato
- ½ cup of sour cream

Directions:

- Melt coconut oil in a saucepan or Dutch oven on medium heat. Cook chicken thighs in a heated pan until just browned.
- Add the onion and green chilies after adding the enchilada sauce and water. Simmer the heat on low, then cover. Cook chicken for 17 to 25 minutes, or until it is soft and thoroughly cooked through, with an internal temperature of at least 165 degrees.
- Remove the chicken with care, then set it on a work surface. If you wish, chop or shred the chicken before adding it back to the saucepan. For an extra 10 minutes of flavor absorption and sauce reduction, let your chicken simmer uncovered.
- Add avocado, cheese, jalapenos, sour cream, tomatoes, and any other preferred toppings before serving. Feel free to alter them to suit your tastes. If preferred, serve over cauliflower rice or alone; just make sure to adjust your individual nutrition information as necessary.

Nutritional values per serving:
Total Calories: 568kcal, **Fat:** 40g, **Carbohydrates:** 6g, **Protein:** 38g

6. White Chicken Chili

Ready in: 45 mins.
Serves: 4
Difficulty: easy
Ingredients:

- 1.5 cups of chicken broth

- 1 lb. of chicken breast
- 2 cloves of garlic, finely minced
- 1 jalapeno, diced
- 1 can of chopped green chiles (4.5oz.)
- 1 green pepper, diced
- 4 tbsp. of butter
- ¼ cup of diced onion
- ¼ cup of heavy whipping cream
- 2 tsp. of cumin
- 4 oz. of cream cheese
- 1 tsp. of oregano
- Salt & Pepper to taste
- ¼ tsp. of cayenne (optional)

Directions:

- Chicken should be seasoned in a big saucepan with cumin, cayenne, oregano, salt, and pepper.
- Golden browning on both sides on medium heat
- Cook chicken for 20 minutes, or until thoroughly done, in a covered saucepan with stock.
- Melt butter in a medium pan as the chicken cooks.
- To a pan, add the chiles, jalapenos, green pepper, and onion. Sauté until the vegetables soften.
- Add the minced garlic, cook for an additional 30 seconds, and then turn off the heat.
- When the chicken is done, shred it with a fork and put it back to the liquid.
- Simmer chicken, stock, and sautéed vegetables in a saucepan for 10 minutes.
- Cream cheese should be heated in a medium bowl until it can be stirred, about 20 seconds.
- Cream cheese and heavy whipping cream are combined.
- Add mixture to the saucepan with chicken and vegetables while briskly stirring.
- Do extra 15 minutes of simmering
- Serve with preferred toppings like sour cream, avocado slices, cilantro, and pepper jack cheese.

Nutritional values per serving:
Total Calories: 481kcal, **Fat:** 30g, **Carbohydrates:** 5g, **Protein:** 39g

7. Lemon Chicken Skewers & Tzatziki Sauce

Ready in: 1 hr. 30 mins.
Serves: 6
Difficulty: easy
Ingredients:
For tzatziki sauce:

- ½ diced European cucumber
- 1 cup of Greek yogurt
- 1 tbsp. of olive oil
- Some garlic powder
- 2 tsp. of lemon juice
- ¼ cup of fresh chopped dill
- Salt & black pepper, freshly ground

For skewers:

- Zest & juice of 1 lemon
- ¼ cup of Greek yogurt
- 1 tsp. of dried oregano
- Some cayenne pepper
- 1 tsp. of garlic powder
- 1½ pounds of skinless, boneless chicken breast cut in half-inch strips
- Salt & black pepper, freshly ground
- Olive oil, as required
- ¼ cup of fresh parsley, chopped

Directions:

- MAKE THE TZATZIKI: Combine the yogurt, cucumber, lemon juice, olive oil, and garlic powder in a medium bowl. Add the dill after seasoning with salt & pepper to taste.
- MAKE SKEWERS: Whisk yogurt with oregano, garlic powder, cayenne, lemon zest, and lemon juice in a small bowl.
- Rub the chicken using the yogurt-lemon mixture to thoroughly coat it in a different bowl.
- Each skewer should have 1 chicken piece on it. To attach the chicken, weave the strip onto the skewer back and forth.
- Olive oil should be brushed on both sides of the skewers before adding salt and pepper. Working in batches, grill or chargrill the food for 4 to 5 minutes on each side or until beautifully browned on both sides.
- Serve right away with tzatziki sauce on the side and parsley as a garnish.

Nutritional values per serving:
Total Calories: 68kcal, **Fat:** 5g, **Carbohydrates:** 3g, **Protein:** 4g

8. Chicken Caprese

Ready in: 30 mins.
Serves: 4
Difficulty: easy
Ingredients:

- Kosher salt & black pepper, freshly ground
- 2 chicken breasts, boneless and skinless
- 1 tbsp. of olive oil
- 1 jar of Pesto (6 oz.)
- 1 tbsp. of butter
- 4-6 slices of fresh mozzarella or six ounces of grated mozzarella cheese
- Balsamic glaze
- 8 cocktails or tomatoes (small), sliced
- Fresh slivered basil

Directions:

- Set the oven up to 400° F.
- Cut the chicken breasts lengthwise with a small, sharp knife. Use black pepper & kosher salt to season both sides. Olive oil & butter are heated over medium-high heat in a large

oven-safe pan. Add the breasts of chicken to the pan when the butter gets melted in the olive oil, being sure not to crowd them. Around 3 to 4 minutes should pass between each side's mild browning and easy removal from the pan.

- Apply a thin layer of basil pesto on each chicken breast, around 1-2 tbsp, per breast. Add a piece of mozzarella & a couple of tomato slices to the top of each chicken breast. Cook the chicken in the oven for 10 to 12 minutes or until it reaches a temperature of 165 degrees, depending on the size of the pan. After taking it out of the oven, top it with some fresh basil and balsamic glaze.

Nutritional values per serving:
Total Calories: 232kcal, **Fat:** 15g, **Carbohydrates:** 5g, **Protein:** 18g

9. Chicken Thighs

Ready in: 4 hrs.
Serves: 4
Difficulty: Medium
Ingredients:

- 1 tbsp. of Za'tar Seasoning
- 2 pounds of Skinless Boneless Chicken Thighs
- 2 ounces of Goat Cheese
- 3 tbsp. of Tahini Paste
- 1/3 cup of Chicken Broth
- 1 tbsp. of Fresh Lemon Juice
- 1/2 Lemon, cut in 2
- 1/2 tsp. of Sea Salt
- Fresh sliced mint to garnish

Directions:

- Place the chicken thighs in the base of the slow cooker after trimming any noticeable big fat pieces of the chicken (optional). Za'atar spice should be sprinkled on and then well rubbed into a chicken to coat it.
- In a medium microwave-safe dish, add the goat cheese. Microwave for 15 to 30 seconds or till the goat cheese just starts to melt. Whisk in the other ingredients (apart from the whole lemon and the mint) until everything is combined smoothly and the cheese has melted.
- Pour over your chicken, covering it completely. The slow cooker should include the two lemon halves.

- For 4-5 hrs. till the chicken is cooked through and tender, cook it covered on low heat or high heat for a couple of hours.
- Pour all of the lemon juice into slow cooker when it has finished cooking. After transferring the chicken to plates, thoroughly combine the left-over sauce in a slow cooker.
- Pour the sauce all over the chicken and, if preferred, top with mint.

Nutritional values per serving:
Total Calories: 596kcal, **Fat:** 35g, **Carbohydrates:** 3g, **Protein:** 63g

10. White Wine Delicious Coq au Vin

Ready in: 55 mins.
Serves: 6
Difficulty: easy
Ingredients:

- Kosher salt & black pepper, freshly ground
- 3 pounds of chicken (breasts, thighs and drumsticks)
- 2 tbsp. of unsalted butter
- 1 sweet onion (large), diced
- 4 strips of bacon, diced
- 3 cloves of garlic, minced
- 2 cups of dry white wine
- 1 pint of sliced cremini mushrooms
- 1 tbsp. of mustard, whole-grain
- ¼ cup of fresh parsley, chopped
- ½ cup of heavy cream

Directions:

- Sprinkle some salt and pepper on the chicken. Melt the butter in a large pan over medium heat. Cook the chicken in the skillet for approximately 4 minutes on each side or until it is thoroughly browned.
- The chicken should be taken out of the pan and put aside. Around 3 minutes after adding the bacon into the pan, the fat will start to render.
- Add the onion & cook for approximately 5 minutes or until transparent. Sauté the mushrooms for 5 to 6 minutes, or until they are soft, after adding the garlic.
- Reintroduce the cooked chicken to the skillet. Over low heat, add the wine to the pan, toss in the mustard, & bring this mixture to a boil.
- During 15 to 20 minutes, with the lid off, the chicken should be nearly completely cooked.
- Remove the skillet's lid and stir in the cream. Cook for 8 to 10 minutes, or till the sauce thickens & the chicken is well cooked.
- Serve right after adding parsley as the garnish.

Nutritional values per serving:
Total Calories: 746kcal, **Fat:** 53g, **Carbohydrates:** 10g, **Protein:** 47g

CHAPTER 4:
Keto Diet - Dinner Recipes
Meat (Lamb, pork, beef) Recipes

1. Lasagna

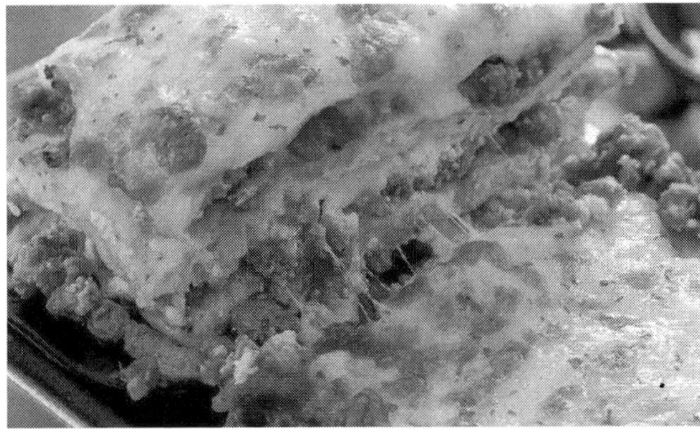

Ready in: 45 mins.
Serves: 8
Difficulty: easy
Ingredients:

- 1 Pound of Ground Beef
- 1 Pound of Mild Italian Sausage, Ground
- ½ Cup of diced onion
- kosher salt & pepper
- 1 tsp. of minced garlic
- 1 Jar of Marinara (24 ounces)
- 2 eggs (large)
- 15 Ounces of Ricotta cheese
- 1 tsp. of Italian seasoning, dried
- 2 Cups of Mozzarella cheese, shredded
- ½ tsp. of minced garlic
- 1 ½ Cups of Parmesan Cheese, Shredded (divided)

Directions:

- Turn the oven on to 375°F.
- Cook the sausage, ground beef, onion, and garlic in a large saucepan over medium-high heat until the meat is browned and crumbled. Add salt and pepper to taste. Add the marinara and stir. Turn off the heat and let the pot alone.
- Combine the ricotta, Italian seasoning, eggs, garlic, & 1 cup of parmesan cheese in a medium separate mixing dish.
- Layer the bottom of a large casserole (9x13) with half of meat mixture. The whole ricotta mixture is layered on top.
- The remaining meat mixture is now placed on top of ricotta mixture.
- Add the mozzarella & the last 1/2 cup of parmesan to complete the dish.
- Bake for 30 minutes in the preheated oven. Before serving, remove it from oven & let it rest for 10 minutes.

Nutritional values per serving:
Total Calories: 568kcal, **Fat:** 41g, **Carbohydrates:** 9g, **Protein:** 41g

2. Beef Tips with Gravy

Ready in: 55 mins.
Serves: 4
Difficulty: easy

Ingredients:

- 1 ½ pounds of sirloin steak in 1.5" cubes
- 1 tbsp. of avocado oil
- 1 tsp. of kosher salt
- 3 tbsp. of butter
- ¼ tsp. of black pepper
- 1 onion (small), diced
- 2 cups of beef broth
- 3 cloves of garlic, minced
- 1 tsp. of xanthan gum
- 2 tbsp. of Worcestershire Sauce
- 2 tbsp. of soy sauce
- 1 tbsp. of Parsley (chopped), for garnish
- ½ tsp. of dried thyme

Directions:

- In a large pan over medium-high heat, warm the avocado oil. Salt and pepper the meat cubes before adding them. Beef should be well browned on both sides before being removed from the pan to a dish and left aside.
- Add the butter into the skillet and lower the heat to medium. Add the chopped onion and stir. Cook for 5 minutes or until transparent. Add the garlic, stir, and cook for another minute. Add the xanthan gum and beef broth, then mix to blend the ingredients. After that, return the steak to the pan and whisk in soy sauce, Worcestershire, and thyme.
- After bringing the liquid to a boil, lower the heat to a simmer. Let it simmer for approximately 30 minutes or until the meat is cooked and the gravy has thickened. Stir occasionally. Add parsley as a finishing garnish.

Nutritional values per serving:
Total Calories: 453kcal, **Fat:** 30g, **Carbohydrates:** 7g, **Protein:** 38g

3. Meatloaf

Ready in: 1 hr. 5 mins.
Serves: 8
Difficulty: easy
Ingredients:

- 1 tbsp. of avocado oil
- 4 slices of keto bread
- 1 Onion (small), diced
- 2 pounds of Ground beef
- 2 tsp. of Minced garlic
- ¼ Cup of fresh parsley, Chopped
- ½ tsp. of Black pepper
- 2 tsp. of Kosher salt
- ¼ Cup of Chicken broth
- 2 Eggs (large)
- 2 tbsp. of Worcestershire sauce
- ¾ Cup of Sugar-free ketchup

Directions:

- Set a sheet pan in the oven at 350 degrees and spray it with cooking oil spray, or you can line it with foil. In a toaster, toast the bread until it is crisp and golden. Cool down. Cut into cubes of 1/2 inch.
- In a small pan over medium heat, warm the avocado oil. When the onion is transparent, add it in. for 8 minutes or so. Cook for a further minute after adding the garlic. Turn off the heat and let the pot alone.

- Add the ground beef, onion, parsley, garlic, salt, chicken stock, pepper, Worcestershire, eggs, and bread cubes to a large mixing bowl. Mix thoroughly.
- Put the mixture onto the baking sheet, then shape it into a uniform loaf. Ketchup should be spread on top.
- Bake for 45–1 hour in a preheated oven or until a meat thermometer registers 165°F.

Nutritional values per serving:
Total Calories: 300kcal, **Fat:** 17g, **Carbohydrates:** 7g, **Protein:** 28g

4. Enchilada Stuffed Delicious Zucchini Boats

Ready in: 40 mins.
Serves: 4
Difficulty: easy
Ingredients:

- Salt & pepper
- 4 Zucchini, medium (6 – 7" long, 2" thick)
- 1 pound of ground beef
- 1 ½ Cup of Shredded Mexican Cheese
- 1 Cup of Enchilada Sauce
- diced tomatoes & cilantro, to garnish (optional)

Directions:

- Set the oven up to 400 degrees Fahrenheit and put foil or silicone baking mat in a sheet pan.
- Each zucchini should be split lengthwise, and the seeds should be removed. Put onto the sheet tray & sprinkle salt and pepper within.
- A big skillet should be heated to medium. When the ground beef cooks in the pan, it breaks apart and crumbles. Add the enchilada sauce once the meat is fully cooked. Turn off the heat and let the pot alone.
- Fill the zucchini boats equally with the meat mixture. Add the cheese on top. The zucchini should be fork-tender after 30 minutes in the oven.

Nutritional values per serving:
Total Calories: 401kcal, **Fat:** 25g, **Carbohydrates:** 10g, **Protein:** 35g

5. Ground Beef Pizza Casserole

Ready in: 30 mins.
Serves: 8
Difficulty: easy

Ingredients:

- ½ diced Onion
- 1 tbsp. of avocado oil
- 1 diced green bell pepper
- 1 pound of Ground beef
- 1 pound of Italian Sausage
- 1 Jar of Marinara
- ½ Cup of Grated parmesan
- 2 Cups of Mozzarella Cheese, Shredded
- ¼ Cup of black olives, sliced (optional)
- 30 slices of Pepperoni

Directions:

- The onions & green peppers should be transparent after being cooked in avocado oil in a big pan over medium heat. (Roughly 5 min.)
- Add your ground meat and sausage, then cut and stir until browned. To taste, add salt & black pepper to the food.
- Remove the meat's oil and throw it away.
- Add the Rao's Marinara Sauce and swirl to incorporate before using a spatula to flatten the top.
- Put both slices of cheese on top, then top with a thick coating of pepperoni.
- Include the olives (optional)
- To brown the top, place the pan in the oven on high broil.
- Serve.

Nutritional values per serving:
Total Calories: 560kcal, **Fat:** 41g, **Carbohydrates:** 8g, **Protein:** 41g

6. Bacon Cheeseburger Casserole

Ready in: 35 mins.
Serves: 8
Difficulty: easy
Ingredients:

- 1 pound of Ground beef
- 1 pound of chopped Bacon into half-inch pieces
- 1 tsp. of Montreal Steak Seasoning
- 1 cup of Heavy cream
- 4 beaten Eggs
- 2 cups of Cheddar Cheese, Shredded

For Sauce:

- ¼ cup of Dill Pickle Relish
- ¼ cup of White vinegar
- ¼ cup of Granular Sweetener
- ½ cup of ketchup, Sugar-free
- ¼ cup of white onion, Minced

Directions:

- Spray cooking spray inside a casserole dish (9x13) and preheat the oven up to 400°F.
- Cook the bacon until it is crisp in a big skillet over medium heat. Using a slotted spoon, remove from skillet & drain onto paper towels. Cook & crumble ground beef for approximately 8 minutes or until it is well cooked. Stir in the steak seasoning after draining the pan's fat.
- Combine all the ingredients in a big mixing basin before pouring them in the casserole dish.
- Put into an oven that has previously been prepared and bake for 25-30 minutes or till well done. Serve.

Nutritional values per serving:
Total Calories: 453kcal, **Fat:** 36g, **Carbohydrates:** 4g, **Protein:** 29g

7. Instant Pot Meatballs

Ready in: 30 mins.
Serves: 38
Difficulty: easy
Ingredients:

- 1/2 pound of Ground Pork lean
- 1 pound of Ground Beef, lean
- 1/4 cup of Distilled White Vinegar
- 1 cup of Tzatziki Sauce
- 3 tbsp. of Olive Oil
- Meatball Mix
- 4 ounces of Red Onion quartered
- 3/4 cup of Rolled Oats
- 1 Egg (large)
- 1/4 cup of Fresh Mint Leaves
- 1 tbsp. of Olive Oil (divided)
- 1 tsp. of Kosher Salt
- 1/2 tsp. of Dried Oregano
- 1/2 tsp. of Ground Cumin
- 1/4 tsp. of Black Pepper, Freshly Ground
- 1/4 tsp. of Ground Cinnamon

Directions:

- Insert meatball in a big food processor bowl, combine the ingredients and pulse until crumbly.
- Pulse the meat in after adding it.
- To the cooking pot of a pressure cooker, add 3 Tablespoons of oil.
- Using a 1.5-inch cookie scoop, shape the meat into balls.
- Place the meatballs and cooking pot in the Instant Pot cooker with care.
- Over the meatballs, pour vinegar.
- Close the pressure valve and lock the lid. Cook for 4 minutes at high pressure.
- Wait 10 minutes after hearing the beep before releasing any residual pressure.
- Lemon juice and zest are used as garnish. Serve with feta cheese and tzatziki sauce.

Nutritional values per serving:
Total Calories: 78kcal, **Fat:** 6g, **Carbohydrates:** 1g, **Protein:** 3g

8. Lamb Chops with Chutney

Ready in: 30 mins.
Serves: 4
Difficulty: easy
Ingredients:
For lamb chops:

- salt & black pepper to taste
- 8 lamb loin chops
- 1 tbsp. of oil
- 1/2 tsp. of dried parsley flakes

For Chutney:

- 1 diced onion
- 1 tsp. of oil
- 6 garlic cloves (minced)
- 1/4 tsp. of chili powder
- 1 red chili, fresh (sliced)
- 1/2 tsp. of turmeric powder
- 1 tsp. of garam masala
- 1/2 tsp. of cumin seeds
- 1 tsp. of sugar
- 2 tomatoes, large (grated or diced)
- 1 tsp. of salt & black pepper

Directions:

- Lamb chops should be washed under cold running water & dried with

paper towels. Add some dried parsley leaves, salt, and pepper.
- Chops should be fried in 1 tbsp of oil for 3 to 5 mins on each side or until golden. Do this in two batches if the pan is tiny; do not cram it. Take them out from the pan after they have finished cooking and set them on a dish to rest.
- In the same pan, put 1 tbsp. Of oil & sauté onion onto medium heat for 4-5 minutes until translucent.
- Add the thinly sliced red pepper and minced garlic, and sauté for an additional two minutes.
- Salt, sugar, pepper, garam masala, turmeric powder, chili powder, cumin seeds, and all of your other spices should be added. Cook on low for two minutes to let the spices warm up.
- Add grated or chopped tomatoes, along with roughly 1/2 cup of water, and simmer for 10 minutes over medium heat. Return the lamb chops to the chutney mixture and serve it over them next. Serve with fresh coriander as a garnish.

Nutritional values per serving:
Total Calories: 461kcal, **Fat:** 23g, **Carbohydrates:** 7g, **Protein:** 51g

9. Lamb Shish Kabobs & Grilled Vegetables

Ready in: 2hr. 25 mins.
Serves: 3
Difficulty: medium
Ingredients:
- 1 yellow onion, small (divided in quarters)
- 1 pound of lamb, cubed (fat trimmed)
- 10 button mushrooms
- 1 large green, orange or red bell pepper (or a mix)

For Marinade:
- ¼ cup of olive oil
- ¼ cup of red wine
- 1 tbsp. of sumac powder
- 1 tsp. of black pepper
- 1 tsp. of salt
- 2 cloves of garlic (minced)
- ¼ tsp. of allspice

Directions:
- Cube your lamb into 1-12" to 2" cubes, cutting off any extra fat before preparing the marinade. Cut the veggies into 2" slices to prepare them.
- Mix the spices, oil, and wine together. Mix in the minced garlic after adding it.
- Lamb and veggies should be marinated before serving. Make sure the contents in the bowl are well coated with the marinade by stirring. Ideally, marinate for at least 2 hrs. or overnight.
- When it's time to grill, switch out the veggies and lamb cubes on metal skewers. There should be at least three skewers with six lamb cubes apiece. Divide the meat between 2 skewers if you're just feeding two people. You may cook the remaining veggies in the grill basket.
- Put the skewers & grill basket on the hot barbeque, cover it, and cook for 8 to 10 minutes total, about 4 to

5 minutes on each side. As you turn the kabobs over, stir the veggies.

- Just before removing the kabobs from the grill, apply more sumac to them.

Nutritional values per serving:
Total Calories: 472kcal, **Fat:** 35g, **Carbohydrates:** 6g, **Protein:** 34g

10. Baked Pork Chops with Onion Gravy

Ready in: 1hr.
Serves: 4
Difficulty: easy
Ingredients:

- 1 tsp. of Sea salt
- 4 8-oz. Boneless pork chops
- 1/2 tsp. of Garlic powder (optional)
- 1/4 tsp. of Black pepper
- 1/2 tsp. of Onion powder (optional)
- 2 tbsp. of Olive oil
- 2 cloves of Garlic (minced)
- 1 Onion, large (sliced in thin half-moons)
- 1 tbsp. of thyme, Fresh (or 1 tsp. of dried thyme)
- 1.5 oz. of Cream cheese (cut in small chunks)
- 1 cup of reduced sodium Chicken broth

Directions:

- Sea salt, onion powder, garlic powder, and pepper should be used to season your pork chops on both sides.
- In a Dutch oven, warm the olive oil over medium-high heat. The pork chops should be seared for 3 minutes total on all sides, without moving, till browned. The pork chops should be moved to a platter and left alone.
- Lower heat to medium-low to medium. Sliced onions should be caramelized for 15 to 20 minutes in the same Dutch oven.
- Heat the oven up to 375 degrees F after the onions are browned (190 degrees C).
- The Dutch oven should now include the minced garlic & thyme leaves. Sauté until aromatic for approximately a minute.
- Dutch oven with chicken broth added. Remove any browned residue from the pan's bottom by scraping. Bring to a mild boil, then decrease the heat and simmer for two to three minutes or until it thickens & the volume is at least cut in half.
- Get rid of the heat. Put the cream cheese in. After the cream cheese has melted, add it and stir until combined.
- Place the pork chops back in the Dutch oven and top with the sauce and onions. Bake for 20 to 25 minutes, or until the food is well cooked, with the cover on. Using a thermometer, check & cook your pork chops to 145 °F (cooking time may vary based on the thickness of the chops (63 degrees C)

Nutritional values per serving:
Total Calories: 541kcal, **Fat:** 35g, **Carbohydrates:** 5g, **Protein:** 48g

SEAFOOD RECIPES

1. Garlic Butter Lemon Shrimp & Zucchini Noodles

Ready in: 10 mins.
Serves: 4
Difficulty: easy
Ingredients:

- 4 zucchini (medium)
- 1 pound of medium raw shrimp (450g), peeled & deveined
- 1 tbsp. of olive oil
- 4 cloves of garlic, finely chopped
- 4 tbsp. of butter (softened), or ghee, divided
- 1 tsp. of Italian seasoning
- Juice of half-fresh lemon
- Some red pepper flakes
- 1/4 cup of vegetable or chicken stock (60ml)
- Salt & freshly cracked black pepper to taste
- Hot sauce (any) to taste
- 1/4 cup of fresh parsley (chopped) for garnish

Directions:

- To prepare the shrimp in lemon garlic butter with zucchini noodles: The zucchini should be washed and its ends trimmed. Use a julienne peeler or spiralizer to create the zucchini pasta, then put it aside.
- In a big skillet over medium-high heat, melt 2 tablespoons of butter and 1 tablespoon of oil. Sprinkle salt and pepper over the layer of shrimp that has been added. Shrimp should be cooked for 1 minute without stirring so that the bottoms are slightly browned.
- To cook the shrimp on the opposite side, toss them for a further minute or two after adding the minced garlic, Italian seasoning, & red pepper flakes. Place the grilled shrimp on a platter with a shallow edge.
- The remaining butter, vegetable or chicken stock, lemon juice, and spicy sauce should all be added to the same pan. For two to three minutes, boil the sauce while stirring often.

- Zucchini noodles should be added and cooked for approximately two minutes while stirring often. If the sauce is too watery, let it decrease slightly. Reintroduce the grilled shrimp, then stir for an additional minute. Shrimp & zucchini noodles should be served right away with lemon slices, more parsley, and pepper. Enjoy!

Nutritional values per serving:
Total Calories: 250kcal, **Fat:** 18g, **Carbohydrates:** 3g, **Protein:** 17g

2. Baked Asparagus Salmon in Foil

Ready in: 20 mins.
Serves: 2
Difficulty: easy
Ingredients:

- 2 tbsp. of chicken broth or vegetable broth
- 1 pound of salmon fillets (450g) divided
- 1 1/2 tbsp. of lemon juice (fresh) or to taste
- 4 tsp. of garlic, minced (4 cloves)
- 1 tbsp. of any hot sauce
- Salt & freshly ground pepper to taste
- 2 tbsp. of freshly chopped cilantro or parsley
- 3-4 tbsp. of butter, diced in small cubes
- 1 lb. of medium asparagus (450g), ends trimmed

Directions:

- To make the foil-wrapped fish for baking in the oven: Turn on the oven to 425°F (220°C). Heavy-duty aluminum foil, cut into 2 sheets of 14 by 12 inches (35 x 30 cm), should be laid out separately on the tabletop. In a small bowl, mix the broth, lemon juice, & spicy sauce.
- Salmon fillets should be salted and peppered on both sides. After dividing the salmon evenly on the aluminum foil in the middle, arrange the trimmed asparagus on a single side of the fish, lining up with the long axis of the foil.
- Add extra salt and pepper to the salmon fillets' seasoning before adding garlic. Over the fillets of salmon and asparagus, liberally drizzle the broth, lemon juice, & spicy sauce combination.
- Distribute butter bits equally among the packets of foil, stacking them on the salmon fillet & asparagus.
- Wrap the ends of the salmon foil packets up once you've crimped the sides together. Keep a little additional room within the wrap so that heat may flow.
- Cook the salmon into the oven, sealed side up, for 9 to 12 minutes or until it is fully cooked. Move the salmon packs to the baking sheet.

- Remove the baked salmon from the foil packets carefully, pour with extra lemon juice, and top with a lemon slice and fresh parsley or cilantro. Enjoy!

Nutritional values per serving:
Total Calories: 610kcal, **Fat:** 39g, **Carbohydrates:** 15g, **Protein:** 51g

3. Creamy Tuscan Salmon

Ready in: 30 mins.
Serves: 3
Difficulty: easy
Ingredients:

- 2 tsp. of olive oil
- 3 fillets of salmon
- 2 tbsp. of butter
- 1 yellow onion (small), diced
- 5 cloves of garlic, finely diced
- 1/3 cup of vegetable broth (80ml)
- 1 3/4 cups of heavy cream
- 5 ounces of sun-dried jarred tomato in oil (150g), drained of oil
- Salt & pepper, to taste
- 1/2 cup of grated Parmesan
- 3 cups of baby spinach leave
- 1 tbsp. of fresh parsley, chopped

Directions:

- In a big skillet over medium-high heat, warm the oil. Salmon filets should be salted and peppered on both sides before being seared for 5 mins on each side or till cooked to your preference in a hot pan with the flesh side down first. Remove the cooked salmon filets from the pan & put them aside.
- Melt the butter into the residual cooking juices in the same pan. Garlic is added, and it is heated until aromatic (about one minute). Stir-fry the added onion until transparent. Sun-dried tomatoes should be added and fried for 1-2 minutes to unleash their flavors. Next, add the veggie broth and let the sauce gradually thicken.
- Stirring periodically, turn the heat down to low, put the heavy cream, & bring to a slow simmer. To your liking, add salt & pepper to the cream sauce.
- Add the parmesan cheese after adding the baby spinach & allowing it to wilt in sauce. After the cheese has melted, let the cream sauce one more minute to boil.
- Re-add the grilled fillets of salmon to the pan, garnish with parsley, and top with the sauce. For Keto dieters, serve the salmon over steamed vegetables or cauliflower rice; for non-Keto dieters, serve it over rice or pasta.

Nutritional values per serving:
Total Calories: 970kcal, **Fat:** 59g, **Carbohydrates:** 17g, **Protein:** 90g

4. Bacon Salmon

Ready in: 25 mins.
Serves: 2
Difficulty: easy
Ingredients:

- 2-6 ounces of filets of Sockeye or salmon
- 2 slices of bacon, diced
- 1 clove of garlic, sliced

- 1 tsp. of olive oil or bacon grease
- 1 ounce of sliced onion (about 1/4)
- 1 tbsp. of tomato paste
- 1/4 cup of vodka
- 1/3 cup of heavy cream
- 1 tbsp. of vodka
- 2 tbsp. of water
- 10 leaves of basil, chiffonade
- salt & pepper to taste
- 1/2 tsp. of lemon zest, grated

Directions:

Preparation:

- On the counter, let the salmon for 15 minutes to reach room temperature. Assemble every element. Slice the bacon into pieces.

Bacon:

- Over medium heat, place a medium frying pan. Stir to coat the bacon with the addition of the bacon & 1 tsp. of bacon fat. Cook for around two minutes. Grate the lemon zest, chiffonade, the basil, & slice the garlic and onion in the meanwhile. Basil should be stacked, rolled lengthwise, cut crosswise, and then sliced into thin ribbons to create chiffonade. Stir the bacon into the pan and let it cook until crisp and browned. Remove the bacon, but keep the pan's grease warm.

Salmon:

- Remove all except approximately 2 tablespoons of the bacon grease from the frying pan, then put the pan back on the stovetop over medium heat.
- Each salmon filet should be very gently salted before being placed on the pan, a nice side up. Depending on the thickness, let the food cook for 3–4 minutes without intervening. The salmon will become lighter once it's been cooked, allowing you to determine when to turn it. Before flipping, you'll want the color shift to be about halfway.
- Flip the fish using a spatula & cook again for approx. 3-4 minutes. To keep warm, transfer the salmon to a platter and lightly tent with a foil wrap.

Sauce:

- Bring the pan back to the burner and maintain the heat at slightly below medium. It will take around 1 1/2 minutes for the onions & garlic to start to soften after being added. While adding the vodka, STEP BACK and carefully remove the pan from the heat. Stirring will help remove the browned parts from the pan's bottom as you reheat it. Reduce the vodka by half.
- To warm and aid in breaking down the tomato paste, add it and mix it in with the onions. Stir in the heavy cream & water after adding them. Let it boil slowly for a minute so that it may slightly thicken. Add the lemon zest, 1 tablespoon of vodka, and the bacon. Stirring the sauce will help to get rid of the strong alcohol scent. Insert the basil. When desired, taste and add a touch of salt and pepper. Turn the heat off.

Plate:

- On a serving platter, put a salmon filet and drizzle half the sauce over it. If desired, add extra basil as a garnish.

Nutritional values per serving:
Total Calories: 431kcal, **Fat:** 19g, **Carbohydrates:** 6g, **Protein:** 38g

5. Salmon Cakes

Ready in: 5 mins.
Serves: 2
Difficulty: easy
Ingredients:

- 1 egg
- 2 pouches of pink salmon (5 oz.)
- ¼ cup of pork rinds, finely ground (optional)
- 2 tbsp. of sarayo (or simple mayo)
- ½ finely chopped jalapeno
- 2 tbsp. of red onion, finely diced
- ¼ tsp. of chili powder
- ¼ tsp. of garlic powder
- 1 tbsp. of avocado oil
- Salt & black pepper to taste

Avocado cream sauce:

- ¼ cup of sour cream
- 1 avocado
- 3 tbsp. of cilantro
- 1-2 tsp. of Water to the required thickness
- 1-2 tbsp. of avocado oil (too thin)
- Salt and black pepper to taste
- Juice of 1/2 lemon

Directions:

- Combine salmon, egg, red onion, jalapeño, sarayo, ground pork rinds, and spice in a large bowl.
- Make patties using the mixture (5-6 small or 4 large)
- Burgers should be cooked for 4-5 minutes on each side, over medium heat, in an oil-drizzled nonstick pan.

Avocado sauce:

- In a food processor, blitz each ingredient until it's smooth.
- Serve hot salmon cakes with avocado sauce & an additional sarayo drizzle.

Nutritional values per serving:
Total Calories: 542kcal, **Fat:** 50g, **Carbohydrates:** 10g, **Protein:** 10g

6. Baked Cod

Ready in: 40 mins.
Serves: 2
Difficulty: easy
Ingredients:

- 1/3 cup of parmesan cheese, finely grated
- 12 ounces of cod, cut into four equal fillets
- 1 tbsp. of fresh parsley, chopped
- 1/4 tsp. of table salt
- 1/2 tsp. of smoked paprika

For Sauce:

- 1/4 cup of dry white wine
- 4 cloves of garlic, minced
- 1 tbsp. of salted butter
- 2 tbsp. of fresh lemon juice

Directions:

- Prepare: Place an oven rack into the center of the oven, & warm to 400 F. Make use of paper towels to pat cod fillets dry. Each fillet should have salt applied on both sides. Set aside.
- Create Sauce: Melt butter on medium heat, stirring frequently, for

less than a minute, in an oven-safe pan. When fragrant and beginning to brown, stir in the minced garlic for 1-2 minutes. Fill the pan with white wine & lemon juice. These should start simmering right away. Stir for a moment, then turn the heat off.

- Add Cod: Mix the parmesan cheese and paprika well in a mixing basin. Put the fish fillets side by side over the sauce in the pan. Spread the parmesan mixture equally on the top of the fillets in the skillet by generously spooning it on top of them. Parmesan that falls off fillets is OK since it will be incorporated into the sauce.
- Bake: Place the pan in the oven once it has reached 400 degrees Fahrenheit. Bake for 15 to 20 minutes or till cod fillets are well done (easily split with a fork).
- Use a spatula to delicately move just the cod fillets to the plates for serving so as not to disturb the parmesan garnish. Pour sauce over fish after combining the remaining liquid in a pan and, if desired, heat it for a minute over medium-high heat to thicken it. Serve immediately after adding parsley to the dish.

Nutritional values per serving:
Total Calories: 280kcal, **Fat:** 9g, **Carbohydrates:** 3g, **Protein:** 36g

7. Pad Thai & Shirataki Noodles

Ready in: 30 mins.
Serves: 2
Difficulty: easy

Ingredients:

- 1 1/2 tbsp. of fish sauce
- 1 package of shirataki fettuccini noodles
- 1 1/2 tbsp. of coconut aminos
- 1/4 tsp. of blackstrap molasses (optional)
- 2 tbsp. of erythritol or xylitol
- 1/8 to 1/4 tsp. of red pepper or cayenne pepper flakes, to taste
- 1-2 tbsp. of coconut oil to cook
- 2-3 tbsp. of fresh lime juice
- 2 minced cloves of garlic
- 2 lightly beaten eggs
- 200 g of fresh chicken or shrimp
- 30 g of bean sprouts

To serve:

- ½ cup of cilantro leaves (fresh), torn
- 3 finely sliced green onions
- lime wedges
- 35 g of peanuts lightly toasted (unsalted), roughly chopped

Directions:

Making the shirataki noodles:

- The noodles should be drained, well-rinsed in cold water, and then boiled for two minutes before being dried in a non-oiled skillet over medium heat. Set aside.

For the Thai keto pad:

- Fish sauce, sugar, coconut aminos, & cayenne or red pepper flakes are well combined in a small dish. Starting with two teaspoons, add lemon juice to taste.
- Over medium heat, warm the oil into a skillet or pan. Garlic is added, and it is gently sautéed until it just

begins to brown. Depending on their size, add the shrimp and fry them for 2 to 5 minutes on each side or till just cooked through. Place the shrimp in a heap along the pan's edge.

- Add the eggs, stirring to scramble them as you cook them until they are firm but still wet and soft.
- Pour the prepared sauce over the shrimp & scrambled eggs, then quickly stir to cover everything. Add the cooked noodles and combine them with the sauce. After adding the soy sprouts, simmer for a further 2-3 minutes.
- Add green onions, cilantro, and peanuts as garnish. Serve immediately, along with fresh lime.

Nutritional values per serving:
Total Calories: 265kcal, **Fat:** 16g, **Carbohydrates:** 5g, **Protein:** 27g

8. Garlic Butter Baked Lobster Tails

Ready in: 15 mins.
Serves: 2
Difficulty: easy
Ingredients:

- 5 cloves of garlic, minced
- 2 (5oz) lobster tails
- ¼ cup of Parmesan (grated), plus some more for serving
- 1 tsp. of Italian seasoning
- Juice of one lemon
- 4 tbsp. of melted butter

Directions:

- Set oven up to 400 degrees Fahrenheit. Combine the garlic, lemon juice, Parmesan, Italian seasoning, melted butter, and salt in a medium bowl.
- Cut the lobster's clear skin with a pair of sharp scissors, then season the tails with garlic butter spice.
- Bake your lobster tails for 12 to 15 minutes after placing them onto a baking sheet coated with parchment paper. The inside lobster flesh will be opaque and solid. It should be between 140 and 145 degrees inside.

Nutritional values per serving:
Total Calories: 515kcal, **Fat:** 36g, **Carbohydrates:** 17g, **Protein:** 34g

9. Tuna Casserole

Ready in: 1 hr.
Serves: 8
Difficulty: easy
Ingredients:

- 2 cups of mushrooms, sliced
- 2 tbsp. of unsalted butter
- 1/2 onion (yellow), chopped
- 1/4 tsp. of pepper
- 1/2 tsp. of kosher salt
- 1 cup of heavy cream
- 1 tsp. of thyme fresh
- 1/2 tsp. of Tabasco
- 2 cups of cabbage shredded
- 1 cup of green beans, diced
- 3 cups of cheddar cheese (sharp), divided
- 3 - 5 oz. cans of albacore tuna, drained
- pork rinds (optional)

Directions:

- Set the oven up to 425 F.

- Over medium heat, add 2 tablespoons of butter to a big heat-safe skillet.
- After the butter has melted, add the 2 cups of sliced mushrooms, 1/2 cup of chopped yellow onions, and 1/2 tsp. Salt and 1/4 tsp. Pepper. Sauté for 10 minutes or until the mushrooms are tender.
- Add 1 cup of heavy cream, 1/2 tsp. of Tabasco, & thyme (1 tsp.). Lower the heat so that the cream just barely simmers (high heat would ruin the cream). Boil vegetables in cream for approximately 15 minutes, or until the white sauce covers the back of a spoon and the cream gets reduced by half.
- Cook in cream with 2 cups of chopped cabbage until wilted, approximately 5 minutes.
- Add cheddar cheese (1 cup), chopped green beans (1 cup), and albacore tuna after taking the pan from the heat (3-4 Oz. Cans drained). To integrate, stir.
- Check the salt level by giving it a taste. Here is when I often add an extra 1/2 teaspoon of salt.
- Add the remaining cheddar on the top (2 cups).
- Heat in a preheated oven for 10-15 minutes, till the casserole is well cooked and the cheese on top begins to bubble.
- Slice the casserole when it has had a chance to cool somewhat.

Nutritional values per serving:
Total Calories: 352kcal, **Fat:** 29g, **Carbohydrates:** 5g, **Protein:** 19g

10. Shrimp & Spinach Cream Sauce

Ready in: 25 mins.
Serves: 4
Difficulty: easy
Ingredients:

- 1 lb. of Shrimp, peeled & deveined
- 2 tbsp. of unsalted Butter
- 1 tsp. of Onion Powder
- 1/2 Cup of Heavy Cream
- 1 tsp. of Garlic Powder
- 1/2 Cup of cubed cream cheese
- 6-8 Cups of Baby Spinach, Fresh
- 1/2 Cup of Water
- Salt & Pepper

Directions:

- In a pan over medium-high heat, melt the butter. Depending on size, add the shrimp to the pan and cook for 2–4 minutes or until just cooked through. Take out and put aside.
- Add heavy cream, cream cheese, water, garlic powder, and onion powder, and reduce heat to medium. Stir until the liquid is smooth and starting to boil.
- Add the spinach and simmer it for 8 to 10 minutes, stirring often, until it wilts. To taste, add salt and pepper.
- Return the shrimp to the pan and serve.

Nutritional values per serving:
Total Calories: 476kcal, **Fat:** 30g, **Carbohydrates:** 18g, **Protein:** 39g

11. Pan Seared Scallops & Lemon Garlic Sauce

Ready in: 40 mins.

Serves: 4
Difficulty: easy
Ingredients:
For Brine:

- 1 cup of hot water
- ⅓ cup of kosher salt
- 1 pound of scallops
- 4 cups of ice cubes

For Scallops:

- 2 tbsp. of unsalted butter
- 2 tbsp. of olive oil
- 1 tbsp. of minced garlic
- 1 tsp. of lemon zest
- 2 tbsp. of lemon juice
- 1 tbsp. of Dijon mustard
- 1 tsp. of chopped dill
- 2 tbsp. of heavy cream
- black pepper, as required for seasoning

Directions:
Brine:

- In a medium dish, combine the salt and the boiling water. Stir till it salt has largely dissolved. When the water is ice cold, add the scallops. Scallops are brined for ten minutes.
- Scallops should be drained and washed in cold water. Move to the sheet pan that has been lined using paper towels. When the scallops are completely dry, put another layer of paper towel above them and gently press. The scallops will sear better if they are drier.
- Before cooking, let scallops remain at room temperature for 10 minutes. Sprinkle a little salt on both sides just before cooking.

Scallops:

- A 12-inch wide pan is heated to medium-high heat. Include olive oil. When the pan is heated, add the scallops in one single layer. Use a spatula to gently push them against the pan, so they come into touch with it. Without moving them, pan-sear them for three minutes or until the surface is golden brown.
- Melt the butter in the pan after adding it. With the pan tilted if necessary, flip the scallops over and use a spatula to baste them with butter. Cook for 1 to 2 minutes or until firm yet tender. Transfer to a plate after turning off the heat.
- Increase the heat to medium-high in the same pan that you used to fry the scallops. Add the garlic and cook for 30 seconds or until fragrant. Lemon juice & lemon zest should be added. After scraping any browned parts from the pan, whisk the ingredients into the sauce and heat for approximately a minute. Whisk in heavy cream and Dijon mustard after removing the pan from the heat. If the sauce needs to be thinner, you may add extra water to it. When needed, taste and add salt and pepper.
- Re-add the scallops to the pan and reheat for 2 minutes on low heat. Serve warm and garnish with finely chopped dill & black pepper.

Nutritional values per serving:
Total Calories: 151kcal, **Fat:** 8g, **Carbohydrates:** 4g, **Protein:** 13g

12. Basil Garlic Butter Steamed Clams

Ready in: 15 mins.
Serves: 4
Difficulty: easy
Ingredients:

- 3 tbsp. of unsalted butter
- 1 pound of clams in shell (steamer-sized), small
- 1 clove of garlic minced
- ½ cup of chicken broth
- 10 basil leaves, whole (fresh)

Directions:

- Over medium heat, melt butter in a large pot with a tight-fitting cover.
- Over medium-high heat, add chicken broth, garlic, and basil leaves to the pot and brings to a boil.
- Clams should be mixed in, and the heat should be kept at medium-high.
- Without taking off the cover, steam for 7-8 minutes.
- Shake pan on heat as clams steam to cover the shellfish evenly.
- Lift the lid; if the sauce seems thin, continue to cook it uncovered until it reaches the required consistency. If it matches your macros, you may add one more tbsp. of butter into the pan.
- When the sauce has the correct consistency, turn off the heat.
- Serve right away and discard any clams which haven't opened.

Nutritional values per serving:
Total Calories: 80kcal, **Fat:** 8g, **Carbohydrates:** 0g, **Protein:** 0g

13. Bacon Crab Stuffed Mushrooms

Ready in: 50 mins.
Serves: 5
Difficulty: easy
Ingredients:

- 12 ounces of lump crab meat, fresh
- 1 pound of cremini mushrooms, large (About 20), cleaned & de-stemmed
- 6 strips of bacon, cooked crisp & crumbled
- ⅓ cup of sharp cheddar cheese, shredded
- 6 ounces of softened cream cheese
- ¼ cup of sour cream
- 3 chopped green onions
- 3 cloves of garlic, minced
- 1 tbsp. of Dijon mustard
- ½ cup of Parmesan cheese, shredded
- sea salt & pepper, to taste

Directions:

- Set the oven up to 400°F. Using a silicone baking mat or parchment paper, line a baking sheet with a rim. (As an alternative, you might use a little muffin pan to support the mushrooms. It will hold them firmly in place and prevent them from toppling over & losing their toppings.
- For ten minutes, bake the mushroom caps. Any extra moisture that collects in the mushroom caps should be poured away. Crab, cream cheese, bacon, cheddar cheese, garlic, sour cream, Dijon, green onions, salt, and pepper should all be

combined in a big mixing basin. Stir well after adding each component.

- Fill each mushroom with the crab mixture. An extra 10 minutes should be baked. Remove from the oven, then sprinkle Parmesan cheese over each mushroom. Bake for 5-10 minutes or until golden brown on top of cheese.

Nutritional values per serving:
Total Calories: 334kcal, **Fat:** 18g, **Carbohydrates:** 6g, **Protein:** 24g

14. Mahi Mahi with Salsa & Feta

Ready in: 45 mins.
Serves: 2
Difficulty: easy
Ingredients:

- 4 tsp. of olive oil, divided
- 2 Mahi Mahi pieces (6 oz.)
- 1/4 cup of diced onion
- 1 tsp. of finely minced garlic
- 1/2 green bell pepper, seeds removed and stem cut out, chopped into half-inch pieces
- 1 tsp. of Greek seasoning
- 1/4 cup of chicken broth
- 1/2 cup of Pace Picante Sauce
- 2 tbsp. of Kalamata olives, sliced
- 2 tbsp. of Feta cheese, crumbled
- salt & freshly ground pepper to taste

Directions:

- In the refrigerator, defrost frozen fish overnight.
- Preheat the oven to 425 F (220 C).
- Give fish some time to warm up.
- Onion & green pepper are sautéed in 2 tablespoons of olive oil over medium to high heat till they begin to turn brown.
- Cook for another minute or two before adding the Greek Seasoning and minced garlic.
- Over medium-low heat, add the homemade chicken stock, salsa, and olives. Simmer for 5–6 minutes or until the sauce has somewhat reduced and thickened.
- Transfer the salsa into a bowl.
- Clean the pan, add the remaining 2 tablespoons of oil, and cook for approximately a minute on medium-high.
- Add the salmon and cook it for two minutes.
- Fish should be turned over and seared for a further two minutes.
- Use non-stick spray or olive oil on a baking dish made of glass or ceramic.
- Put the seared fish into the baking dish, top with salsa, and bake for six minutes.
- After taking it out of the oven, top it with crumbled Feta.
- Serve warm.

Nutritional values per serving:
Total Calories: 352kcal, **Fat:** 15g, **Carbohydrates:** 10g, **Protein:** 43g

15. Fish Pie

Ready in: 1 hr. 15 mins.
Serves: 6
Difficulty: easy
Ingredients:

- 1 cauliflower, Large
- 4 eggs, large

- 1/4 cup of butter or ghee, + 2 tbsp.
- 2 fillets of skinless salmon, preferably wild
- 2-3 fillets of white fish like cod or haddock, skinless
- 2 fillets of skinless mackerel
- 2 bay leaves
- 1 red onion, medium
- 4 garlic cloves
- 1/2 cup of water
- 1 cup of heavy whipping cream
- 1 tsp. of Dijon mustard
- 1 cup of cheddar cheese (+ 1/2 cup), shredded
- 1/8 tsp. of ground nutmeg
- 4 tbsp. of chives, freshly chopped
- sea salt & ground pepper, to taste
- fresh parsley or some more chives to garnish

Directions:

- Cooking the eggs comes first. Water should fill a tiny saucepan to the top third. Be sure to season with salt. By doing this, the eggs won't break. Bring up to a boil. Each egg should be dipped in & out of boiling water with a spoon or your hand. Take caution not to burn yourself. As a result of the less abrupt temperature drop, the egg won't break. The eggs should be hard-boiled for about 10 minutes. For big eggs, this period is effective. When finished, take the food off the heat and put it in a bowl of ice water. Set the peeled eggs aside.
- Make the topping of cauliflower. Cut the cauliflower head into tiny florets after washing. Put in a saucepan with approximately 2 inches of water poured on a steaming rack. Ten minutes after bringing to a boil, continue cooking. Avoid overcooking. Put the cooked cauliflower, 1/4 cup butter, and 1/4 teaspoon salt in a blender. Process till creamy and smooth. Set aside when.
- The fish is poached. Set the oven to 425 °F/220 °C. The skin of the fillets doesn't have to be removed for mackerel, which may be diced into medium-sized (5 cm or roughly 2 inches) pieces instead. Pour the cream & water over the fish into a deep pan.
- The onion should be peeled, diced small, and added to the pan with bay leaves & cloves. Add 1/4 teaspoon salt, bring to a boil, and then simmer for 8 to 10 minutes on low heat.
- Transfer the fish onto a baking dish that is deep enough to accommodate the fish & cauliflower topping using a slotted spoon.
- Get the sauce ready. The fish and cream sauce should be simmering over medium heat. The last 2 tbsp. of butter should be added.
- Include Dijon mustard and nutmeg. For approximately 5 minutes, simmer or until it begins to thicken. Turn the heat off. Get rid of the spices (whole cloves & bay leaves if used). After the cheese has melted and thickened, add 1 cup of cheddar that has been chopped.
- The fish pie is layered. Halve & quarter the eggs & arrange them

into the baking dish above the cooked fish. Over the eggs & fish, pour the cream and cheese sauce.

- Put some spring onions or chopped chives on top. Add the mashed cauliflower on top. Make a beautiful design with the fork tines on top.
- Add the last 1/2 cup of the shredded cheddar on top before baking. Sauté for 30 to 35 minutes or until golden brown on top.
- After finishing, shut off the oven, then leave the food on a wire rack to cool for 15 minutes. While the fish pie is hot, the sauce will be liquid; but as it cools, the sauce will thicken. Serve warm or let to cool before storing in the refrigerator for up to five days.

Nutritional values per serving:
Total Calories: 616kcal, **Fat:** 46g, **Carbohydrates:** 8g, **Protein:** 37g

16. Coconut Spinach Fish Curry

Ready in: 25 mins.
Serves: 6
Difficulty: easy
Ingredients:

- 2-4 tbsp. of curry powder/paste of choice
- 1 kg of firm white fish in cubes
- 400 ml of coconut cream
- 500 g of spinach, washed & sliced
- 400 ml of water

Directions:

- The curry paste should be heated for two to three minutes over moderate heat to bring out the flavor of the spices.
- Bring to a boil after adding the water and coconut cream.
- Reduce the heat before adding the fish pieces. For 10 to 15 minutes, simmer.
- After the spinach has wilted, add the prepped spinach and simmer for a further 3–4 minutes.
- Serve in large dishes.

Nutritional values per serving:
Total Calories: 405kcal, **Fat:** 26g, **Carbohydrates:** 7g, **Protein:** 38g

17. Baked Halibut with Parmesan, Sour Cream and Dill

Ready in: 35 mins.
Serves: 2
Difficulty: easy
Ingredients:

- salt & black pepper (freshly ground), to taste
- 2 pieces of halibut or any other white mild fish, thawed if frozen & dried with paper towels
- 3 tbsp. of sour cream
- 1/4 tsp. of dill weed (dried
- 1/4 tsp. of garlic powder
- 2 tbsp. of Parmesan cheese, finely ground
- 3 tbsp. of green onion, sliced

Directions:

- Halibut should be defrosted overnight in the fridge, then put in a baking dish and dried with paper towels.
- As you prepare the other ingredients, let the halibut warm up to room temperature. Turn the oven on to 375°F/190°C.

- 3 tbsp. of green onions should be thinly sliced, and 2 tbsp. Should be chopped. To decorate the finished meal, save the remaining 1 tbsp of sliced onions.
- Mix the garlic powder, sour cream, and dill weed in a small bowl. Green onions and Parmesan cheese that has been finely shredded are added.
- After the fish has reached room temperature, utilize a rubber scraper to evenly distribute the topping mixture over each piece of fish.
- Fish should be baked until it achieves an internal temperature of 145°F (62°C) or until the chunks are firm to the touch but not hard. (Press down with a fork to test.)
- Serve hot with the remaining green onions, sliced.

Nutritional values per serving:
Total Calories: 290kcal, **Fat:** 12g, **Carbohydrates:** 3g, **Protein:** 40g

18. Tuna Melts with Tomato Halves

Ready in: 25 mins.
Serves: 2
Difficulty: easy
Ingredients:

- 1 can of light tuna (flaked) in water
- 2 tomatoes (large)
- 2 tbsp. of mayo
- 1/2 cup of cheddar cheese
- 2 - 4 tbsp. of green onion, chopped
- 2 sliced pickles
- 4 slices of avocado
- 4 pieces of bacon, cooked
- salt and black pepper to taste

Directions:

- The oven temperature should be 400 degrees. Cut the tomato in half, then remove the seeds. While it's not necessary, if the seeds are left in, the mixture may get sloppy. Alternatively, you could simply use thick tomato slices.
- Open the tuna can, pour the contents into a bowl, then top with the mayo and green onions. To blend, stir. Instead, you may just spray the mayo on top.
- On a baking sheet with parchment paper, arrange the tomatoes. Place half of the tuna mix per tomato half. Each tomato half should have cheese on top, followed by pickle slices.
- Bake for about 15 minutes or till cheese is melted & bubbling. Serve immediately after removing from the oven.

Nutritional values per serving:
Total Calories: 465kcal, **Fat:** 36g, **Carbohydrates:** 7g, **Protein:** 28g

19. Shrimp Lettuce Wraps

Ready in: 2 hrs. 20 mins.
Serves: 8
Difficulty: medium
Ingredients:
For Thai Shrimp:

- 1 ½ tbsp. of Thai Seasoning Paste
- 1 lb. of shrimp deveined, peeled, tails removed
- 1 tsp. of Chili Pepper Paste

- Half a head of iceberg lettuce, split into leaves
- 2 tbsp. of olive oil or butter
- ½ cup of chopped tomatoes

Lime Cilantro Mayo:

- Salt & pepper to taste
- ¼ cup of mayonnaise
- ½ tsp. of garlic paste
- 1 tbsp. of cilantro paste
- Salt & pepper to taste
- 2 tbsp. of fresh lime juice

Directions:

- Mix shrimp with chili pepper paste and Thai spice paste in a medium bowl. For one to two hours, marinate covered in the fridge.
- A big skillet is warmed up over medium-high heat. Swirl in some butter or oil to coat. Put the shrimp in one single layer & heat for 2 minutes. Then toss and cook for an additional 1 to 2 minutes or until the shrimp are fully cooked.
- 8 lettuce leaves should each have one shrimp (4 - 5 shrimp per leaf, based on the size of the shrimp). Add some tomato chunks & season to taste.

Lime Cilantro Mayo:

- Mayonnaise, garlic paste, cilantro paste, lime juice, salt, and pepper should all be combined in a small bowl. Stir well, then pour over the shrimp.

Nutritional values per serving:
Total Calories: 268kcal, **Fat:** 18g, **Carbohydrates:** 6g, **Protein:** 16g

20. Bacon Wrapped Lobster

Ready in: 1 hr.
Serves: 2
Difficulty: easy
Ingredients:
For Main Dish:

- 9-10 bacon strips
- 1 lb. of lobster tail
- 4 stalks of green onion (in 2" segments)
- 2 tbsp. of butter (plus some more for dipping)
- 1 tbsp. of olive oil
- 1 tsp. of garlic powder
- 1 tsp. of red pepper flakes
- 1 tsp. of paprika
- ½ tsp. of celery salt
- Salt & pepper to taste
- ½ tsp. of cayenne pepper

For Dipping Sauce:

- 1 egg
- 2 cloves of garlic
- 1 tbsp. of lemon juice
- ½ tsp. of salt

- 1 tbsp. of chopped parsley
- ½ cup of olive oil
- pinch of pepper

Directions:

- Take the lobster flesh out of the tail shell, and cook it for approximately five mins on each side in an oiled pan over medium heat.
- Put two tbsp. of butter in the pan & let it melt halfway through the cooking. Sprinkle salt and spices over the lobster after letting it soak into the butter on both sides.
- After frying, remove the lobster from the heat and chop into portions between 1 and 1/2 inches. Cutting along the direction of the tail's natural grooves is beneficial.
- Cut each bacon strip in half with your hands (ending up with two strips half as long).
- Roll a piece of bacon from one end to the other while adding a lobster piece & a few green onion bits. Use a toothpick to secure it.
- Place each piece on a prepared baking sheet, leaving space between them to allow for air circulation. The bacon-wrapped pieces shouldn't be in close proximity to one another.
- Put it in the oven with the second-highest broil setting. After 8 to 10 minutes of broiling, flip each one over. Watch out for that bacon!

Garlic Aioli Dip:

- While the main dish is broiling, combine 1 egg, 2 cloves of raw or roasted garlic, 1 tablespoon of lemon juice, and 1 tablespoon of parsley that has been minced, salt, and pepper in a food processor.
- Mix until the garlic is completely smooth and the egg has diminished in color.
- 1/2 cup olive oil should be added very gradually while the blender is running. Pouring the oil in should take three minutes to obtain the ideal consistency.
- Remove the oven pan and place the lobster pieces on a serving plate after the bacon is completely crispy on both sides. Serve the pieces with melted butter and garlic aioli. Squeeze some lemon juice over each piece. To prepare a sweet and smoky dip, melt butter with salt & paprika.

Nutritional values per serving:
Total Calories: 200kcal, **Fat:** 3g, **Carbohydrates:** 0g, **Protein:** 4g

CHAPTER 5:
Keto Diet - Appetizers, Snacks & Sides
Appetizers

1. Stuffed Mushrooms

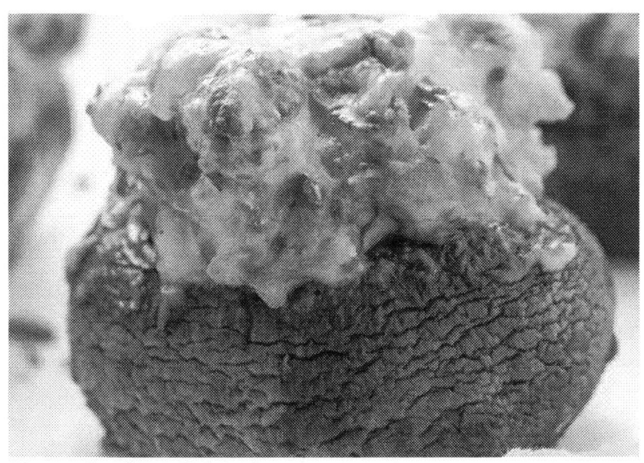

Ready in: 55 mins.
Serves: 6
Difficulty: easy
Ingredients:

- 5 slices of Bacon
- 1 lb. of Cremini mushrooms (removed stems)
- 4 cloves of Garlic (minced)
- 4 oz. of Cream cheese (in small chunks)
- 3/4 lb. of Italian sausage, Ground
- 2 tbsp. of Fresh parsley
- 1/4 cup of parmesan cheese, Grated
- 1/2 cup of shredded Mozzarella cheese (divided)

Directions:

- Set the oven up to 400 degrees Fahrenheit. Use foil or parchment paper to line a sheet pan.
- On the sheet pan, arrange the mushroom caps, open side up, with space among them. Set aside.
- Place the bacon on a large, cold pan in a single layer. Cook for about 10 min over medium heat, stirring periodically, until browned & crispy. While keeping the bacon oil in the pan, remove cooked bacon to a dish lined with paper towels and put it aside.
- To the skillet, add the minced garlic. On medium heat, sauté for approximately a minute or until aromatic.
- Sausage ground is added. Heat up to a medium-high setting. Simmer for 8 to 10 minutes, stirring and breaking up with a spatula, until browned and well cooked. Grease from skillet should be drained.
- After everything is well combined, add the fresh parsley, cream cheese, 1/4 cup mozzarella, & 1/4 cup parmesan.
- Crumble or chop the bacon. The sausage mixture after stirring.
- Fill the mushroom caps to the brim with the sausage filling.
- 3/4 teaspoon of the remaining 1/4 cup of mozzarella should be placed on top of each mushroom. To make the cheese stick, press it into the tops.

- For 10 minutes, bake the keto-stuffed mushrooms till the cheese is golden.
- When the mushrooms are tender, cover the top with foil, making sure it doesn't contact the cheese. Bake for an additional 10 minutes.

Nutritional values per serving:
Total Calories: 393kcal, **Fat:** 30g, **Carbohydrates:** 6g, **Protein:** 20g

2. Bacon Wrapped Asparagus

Ready in: 30 mins.
Serves: 6
Difficulty: easy
Ingredients:

- 12 slices of Bacon
- 24 stalks of Asparagus (trimmed)
- 1 tsp. of Olive oil
- 1/4 tsp. of Black pepper
- 1/4 tsp. of Garlic salt

Directions:

- Set the oven up to 400 degrees Fahrenheit (204 degrees C). Put a greased or non-stick oven-safe wire rack on a cookie sheet.
- Trim the asparagus's woody ends. Add a drizzle of olive oil. Add to taste some black pepper and garlic salt. Only enough oil is required to ensure that the salt & pepper have adhered to the food.
- For thinner strips, slice the bacon lengthwise. Each bacon strip should be snugly wrapped around the asparagus stalk, with the bacon barely marginally overlapping on each stalk. Put seam side down on the wire rack.
- For ten minutes, bake. Turn over with tongs. Bake the bacon for a further 5 to 10 minutes or until nearly crispy. Preheat the oven up to broil, then put under the broiler for 2 mins to crisp up further.

Nutritional values per serving:
Total Calories: 202kcal, **Fat:** 18g, **Carbohydrates:** 3g, **Protein:** 6g

3. Zucchini Chips

Ready in: 15 mins.
Serves: 4
Difficulty: easy
Ingredients:

- 1 tbsp. of Olive oil
- 1 Zucchini (medium)
- 1/8 tsp. of Black pepper
- 1/4 tsp. of Sea salt

Directions:

- Slice the zucchini into 1/8-inch thick slices using a mandoline.
- Using a paper towel, pat any extra moisture from the zucchini slices.
- Set the air fryer up to 325 degrees Fahrenheit (162 degrees C).
- The zucchini slices, sea salt, olive oil, and pepper should all be combined in a medium bowl. Once all of the slices are coated, toss.
- In the air fryer, arrange the slices of zucchini in a single layer. For 8 to 12 minutes, cook. After eight minutes, check the slices and take out any that are browning or crisping. Check until all of the slices are done, continuing to check every few minutes. Repeat with the remaining

zucchini slices. During cooling, zucchini will become more pliable.

Nutritional values per serving:
Total Calories: 39kcal, **Fat:** 3g, **Carbohydrates:** 1g, **Protein:** 0g

4. Cucumber Smoked Salmon Bites

Ready in: 15 mins.
Serves: 10
Difficulty: easy
Ingredients:

- 1/4 cup of Greek yogurt (Full-fat)
- 6 oz. of Cream cheese (softened)
- 1/4 tsp. of Garlic powder
- 1 English cucumber, large (sliced diagonally, ¼" thick)
- 2 tbsp. of Fresh chopped dill (plus some more for garnishing)
- 4 oz. of Smoked salmon (thinly sliced & cut in pieces)

Directions:

- Mash the Greek yogurt, cream cheese, and garlic powder together in a small bowl. Add the fresh dill and stir.
- Fill a piping bag with the cream cheese mixture.
- Place the cucumber slices on a dish in a single layer. Each slice of cucumber should have roughly 1/2 spoonful of the mixture of cream cheese on it. Add a slice of folded-over smoked salmon on top. If desired, add more dill as a garnish.

Nutritional values per serving:
Total Calories: 80kcal, **Fat:** 6g, **Carbohydrates:** 2g, **Protein:** 3g

5. Taco Cups

Ready in: 15 mins.
Serves: 8
Difficulty: easy
Ingredients:

- Cookie sheet
- 1 cup of cheddar cheese, shredded

Fillings:

- Keto-friendly as required

Directions:

- Set the oven to 350 degrees.
- The simplest method to make them is to use a cupcake pan and cookie sheet topped with a silicone baking mat. If you aren't using silicone, use a non-stick cooking oil spray to coat the cookie sheet & cupcake pan for simple cheese cup removal.

- Cheddar cheese shreds should be used to create eight circles on a cookie sheet, ideally one lined with a silicone baking mat. Each circle should be about 3 1/2" in diameter and be created with 2 tbsp of cheese.
- Bake the cookie sheet in the preheated oven for 5-7 minutes or until the edges are starting to brown.
- After the baking sheet has cooled for ten seconds, gently take each cheese circle & set it inside the muffin pan slot to create a cup.
- Before gently removing the Taco Cups from the muffin tin and adding the preferred contents, allow the cups to cool in the pan for 10 minutes at least.

Nutritional values per serving:
Total Calories: 56kcal, **Fat:** 4g, **Carbohydrates:** 0g, **Protein:** 3g

6. Cauliflower Wings

Ready in: 30 mins.
Serves: 6
Difficulty: easy
Ingredients:

- 3 beaten eggs
- 1 head of cauliflower
- ¾ cup of almond flour
- 1 tsp. of garlic powder
- ¾ cup of Parmesan cheese, finely grated
- Salt & Pepper to taste
- ½ tsp. of smoked paprika

For Sauce:

- 4 tbsp. of butter
- 1 cup of Red Hot Sauce

Directions:

- Your oven or air fryer should be preheated to 420 degrees.
- Cut the cauliflower into bigger florets after coring it.
- In a small bowl, combine the eggs and beat them.
- Almond flour, garlic powder, Parmesan, smoked paprika, salt, and pepper should all be combined in a different bowl.
- Before coating with the almond flour mixture, dip the cauliflower in the egg mixture.
- Once you are ready to cook, transfer to a baking sheet lined with paper.
- The remaining cauliflower should be continued.
- Put some oil on the baking sheet with parchment paper or the bottom of the air fryer.
- Cauliflower should be added in one single layer. Spray the top.
- Fry until golden brown, turning halfway through, for 10-12 minutes in an air fryer or for 20-22 minutes in the oven.

For Sauce:

- Hot Sauce and butter are combined in a small skillet to produce the sauce whilst cauliflower is cooking.
- Melt the butter by heating it over medium-low heat.

To Combine:

- Use a slotted spoon to serve the sauce-coated crispy cauliflower.

Nutritional values per serving:
Total Calories: 257kcal, **Fat:** 20g, **Carbohydrates:** 9g, **Protein:** 13g

7. Cheesy Garlic Bread

Ready in: 15 mins.
Serves: 2
Difficulty: easy
Ingredients:

- 1/2 cup of shredded mozzarella cheese
- 1 egg
- 1 tbsp. of parmesan cheese
- 1/4 tsp. of baking powder
- 3/4 tsp. of coconut flour
- 1/8 tsp. of Italian Seasoning
- 1 tbsp. of butter, melted
- Some salt
- 1/4 tsp. of garlic powder
- 1/4 tsp. of basil seasoning
- 1/2 cup of shredded mozzarella cheese

Directions:

- A 400-degree oven is recommended. Let the Waffle Maker heat up by plugging it into the wall. Grease the waffle machine lightly.
- In a small bowl, add the first 7 ingredients and whisk to blend thoroughly.
- Close the waffle maker after sprinkling half the batter on it. Sauté until golden brown, about 3 to 4 minutes.
- Repeat for the remaining batter after gently removing the bread from the Waffle Maker.
- Melt the butter & add the garlic powder to a small bowl.
- Place each piece of bread on a baking sheet, cut in half (or thirds), and then brush the tops using the garlic butter mixture.
- Add mozzarella cheese on top and bake for 4 to 5 minutes.
- To get the cheese to bubble and become golden brown, set the oven to broil & transfer the baking pan to the highest shelf for a minute or two. Broiling may cause it to burn fast, so watch it extremely carefully.
- Remove from oven, then top with basil seasoning. Enjoy!

Nutritional values per serving:
Total Calories: 270kcal, **Fat:** 21g, **Carbohydrates:** 3g, **Protein:** 16g

8. Soft Pretzel Bites

Ready in: 30 mins.
Serves: 10

Difficulty: easy

Ingredients:

- 1 oz. of Cream Cheese
- 2 cups of Part-Skim, Low Moisture, shredded Mozzarella Cheese
- 2 Eggs
- 1 tbsp. of Yeast
- 1 ½ cups of Almond Flour
- 2 tbsp. of Low Carb Sweetener
- Pretzel Salt
- 1 tbsp. of Baking Powder

Directions:

- Set the oven to 400 degrees Fahrenheit & line the baking sheet using a silicone baking mat or parchment paper.
- Combine the cream cheese and mozzarella cheese in a large basin. Once the cheeses get melted & readily combined, microwave them at 30-second intervals, rotating after each one.
- Add almond flour, sweetener, yeast, and baking powder. Save the second egg for last. All the components should be well mixed.
- Create four equal pieces of dough. Roll each part of the dough into a piece that is 13 to 14 inches long. Cut the rolled-out material into pieces measuring 1-1 12". With approximately 1" between each piece, arrange the cut sections on the prepared baking sheet. With the remaining dough, repeat.
- The last egg should be beaten in a mixing bowl. Brush the beaten egg onto the pretzel pieces' tops with a pastry brush before finishing with pretzel salt.
- Bake for 10 to 12 minutes, or until golden brown, in a preheated oven. Before serving, take them out of the oven and let them cool for three to five minutes.

Nutritional values per serving:

Total Calories: 188kcal, **Fat:** 15g, **Carbohydrates:** 5g, **Protein:** 11g

9. Spinach Feta Pinwheels

Ready in: 1 hr.

Serves: 16

Difficulty: easy

Ingredients:

For Mozzarella Dough:

- 2 tsp. of baking powder
- 1/2 cup of coconut flour
- 3/4 tsp. of xanthan gum
- 2 eggs (large)
- 12 ounces of pre-shredded mozzarella cheese (part-skim)

For pinwheels:

- 3/4 cup of feta cheese, crumbled (about three ounces)
- 8 ounces of frozen spinach (chopped), thawed & drained
- 1/4 cup of grated Parmesan cheese (about one ounce)
- 1/2 tsp. of marjoram, dried (or 1/4 tsp. of dried oregano)
- 2 cloves of garlic, minced
- 1/2 tsp. of salt
- 1 tbsp. of butter (unsalted), melted
- 1/2 tsp. of black pepper
- Coarse sea salt to sprinkle

Directions:

For Dough:

- Use a big piece of parchment paper or a silicone baking mat to line a work area. Mix the baking powder, coconut flour, and xanthan gum in a medium bowl. Set aside.

- Heat the cheese in a large microwave-safe dish in 30-second bursts on high until nearly liquid. Use a rubber spatula for kneading the dough in the bowl after adding the eggs and flour mixture.
- When the dough is cohesive, spread it out on the prepared work area & continue to knead it. As you're making the filling, set the dough aside.

To make the pinwheels:

- Bake at 375 degrees Fahrenheit & line the baking sheet with parchment paper or a silicone baking mat.
- The spinach should be squeezed to remove as much moisture as possible before being put in a medium bowl. Add the feta, Parmesan, marjoram, garlic, salt, and pepper after thoroughly combining.
- Transfer the prepped dough to a wide parchment paper piece or similar baking surface that has been lightly greased. Put another waxed or parchment paper piece on top after patting it into a rough square.
- The dough is rolled out into a 16-inch square. Leaving a half-inch border around the edge, spread the filling on top. Wrap up the dough firmly & pinch the border to seal.
- Slice the dough into 1-inch rounds with a very sharp knife, then arrange the pinwheels cut-side down on the preheated baking sheet. Add some coarse salt and butter after brushing.
- Bake the pinwheels for 18-22 minutes or until they are lightly browned and spring back when touched. Remove from the oven, and allow the pan cool fully.

Nutritional values per serving:
Total Calories: 114kcal, **Fat:** 7g, **Carbohydrates:** 4g, **Protein:** 8g

10. Buffalo Chicken Delicious Celery Sticks

Ready in: 55 mins.
Serves: 32
Difficulty: easy
Ingredients:

- ½ cup of butter
- ½ cup of hot sauce

- 1 tbsp. of white vinegar
- ¼ tsp. of cayenne pepper
- ¼ tsp. of Worcestershire sauce
- 1 clove of garlic crushed
- 2 tbsp. of cream cheese
- ¼ tsp. of salt
- 1 lb. of chicken (cooked), shredded
- Ranch (optional)
- 1 bunch of celery in 2-3" long pieces
- Green onions (optional)

Directions:

- Combine butter, hot sauce, vinegar, cayenne, Worcestershire, garlic, and salt in a medium-sized skillet over medium heat.
- While whisking continuously, bring the ingredients to a boil. Cream cheese should be added after the sauce has reached a rolling boil till mixed, whisk.
- Shredded chicken should be added to the sauce & mixed until coated.
- Add one to two teaspoons of buffalo chicken to each celery stick. Ranch dressing should be drizzled on each stick before adding green onions. Enjoy!

Nutritional values per serving:
Total Calories: 64kcal, **Fat:** 5g, **Carbohydrates:** 0g, **Protein:** 3g

SNACKS

1. Jalapeno Poppers

Ready in: 25 mins.
Serves: 12
Difficulty: easy
Ingredients:

- 1/4 cup of shredded Cheddar cheese
- 6 Jalapeno peppers, medium (sliced lengthwise & seeds removed)
- 3 oz. of Cream cheese (softened)
- 2 cloves of Garlic (minced or crushed)
- 1/4 cup of chopped Green onions
- 6 slices of bacon, Cooked (crumbled)
- 1 tbsp. of cilantro, Fresh (chopped)

Directions:

- Set the oven up to 400 degrees Fahrenheit (204 degrees C). Put foil or parchment paper on a baking pan.
- Mix or mash the cream cheese, cheddar cheese, cilantro, green onions, and garlic in a small bowl. If cream cheese is just too firm, you may boil it a little.
- Put the mixture into the jalapeno halves. Put the baking sheet with the liner.
- About 1/2 tbsp. of crumbled bacon should be placed on top of each jalapeño pepper, gently pushing it into cream cheese filling.
- Bake the peppers for approximately 15 minutes or until they are tender and the bacon is crisp on top.

Nutritional values per serving:
Total Calories: 56kcal, **Fat:** 4g, **Carbohydrates:** 1g, **Protein:** 2g

2. Chicken Nuggets

Ready in: 25 mins.
Serves: 4
Difficulty: easy
Ingredients:

- 1/4 cup of Mayonnaise
- 2 Boneless & skinless medium chicken breasts

- 1 tsp. of White vinegar
- 1/2 tsp. of Sea salt (plus some more for brine)
- 1 cup of Almond Flour
- 2 tbsp. of Olive oil
- 1/4 tsp. of Black pepper

Directions:

- Several teaspoons of sea salt should be added to a sizable basin of water. Put the chicken in salt water and brine it for a minimum of 10 minutes and a maximum of an hour. Drain and pat yourself dry. Chicken should be cut into nugget-sized pieces.
- Combine the mayonnaise & vinegar in a small bowl.
- In another dish, combine the almond flour along with some sea salt & black pepper. You are welcome to add any other seasonings you choose.
- Apply a thin coating of the mixture of mayonnaise per piece of chicken before pressing it into the mixture of almond flour.

FRYING:

- In a skillet set over medium-high heat, warm the oil. (Use substantial amounts of oil in each batch—at least 2 teaspoons (30 mL)). Batch-cook the nuggets in one single layer for 2-3 minutes on each side or until golden.

BAKING:

- Set the oven up to 450 degrees Fahrenheit (232 degrees C). Chicken nuggets should be arranged in a single layer on a baking sheet lined with parchment paper. Bake for 6 to 8 minutes or until golden brown on the bottom. Flip carefully, then bake it for a further 6 to 8 minutes or until well done.

Nutritional values per serving:
Total Calories: 324kcal, **Fat:** 26g, **Carbohydrates:** 6g, **Protein:** 18g

3. Cheese Ball with Bacon, Cream Cheese & Green Onion

Ready in: 10 mins.
Serves: 16
Difficulty: easy
Ingredients:

- 3/4 cup of shredded Cheddar cheese
- 16 oz. of Cream cheese (softened)
- 3/4 cup of Bacon bits
- 1/4 cup of Pecans (chopped)
- 1/4 cup of Green onions (chopped)

Directions:

- Use a powerful blender, food processor, stand mixer along with a paddle attachment, or a hand mixer to combine the cream cheese & cheddar cheese.
- The cheese should be rolled into a ball, covered completely with plastic wrap, and chill until solid, about one to two hours.
- Mix the bacon bits, pecans, and green onions in a medium bowl. In the mixture, roll the cheese ball.
- Wrap plastic wrap firmly around the ball. Keep chilled until you're ready to serve.

Nutritional values per serving:
Total Calories: 159kcal, **Fat:** 14g, **Carbohydrates:** 1g, **Protein:** 6g

4. Buffalo Chicken Wings

Ready in: 50 mins.
Serves: 6
Difficulty: easy
Ingredients:
For wings:

- 2 tsp. of Baking powder
- 3 lbs. of Chicken wings (flats & drumettes)
- 1/4 tsp. of Black pepper
- 1 tsp. of Sea salt

For buffalo sauce:

- 1/4 cup of butter, unsalted (melted)
- 1/2 cup of Buffalo sauce

For serving: (optional)

- Celery sticks
- Blue cheese dressing (for dipping)

Directions:

- Set the oven up to 400 degrees Fahrenheit (204 degrees C). Put 2 lined baking sheets within 2 oven-safe racks.
- You should put the chicken wings in a big bowl. Add salt, pepper, and baking powder, then toss to coat.
- Place wings in one single layer on the racks. Bake for 40 to 45 minutes or until the skin is crisp and the interior temperature reaches 165 °F (74 degrees C).
- Buffalo sauce & melted butter should be mixed together in a large basin at the end of baking. Add the finished wings to the bowl & mix in the sauce.
- Serve with celery sticks & blue cheese dressing.

Nutritional values per serving:
Total Calories: 341kcal, **Fat:** 27g, **Carbohydrates:** 0g, **Protein:** 22g

5. Nachos with Spicy Chicken

Ready in: 30 mins.
Serves: 4
Difficulty: easy
Ingredients:

- 1 1/2 cups of chicken breast, Cooked (without seasonings; shredded or diced)
- 1 1/2 cups of shredded Cheddar cheese
- 1/2 Avocado, large (diced)
- 3 tbsp. of White minced onion
- 1/2 cup of diced Roma tomato
- 1 tsp. of Paprika
- 1/2 tsp. of Cumin
- 1/2 tsp. of Garlic salt
- 1/4 cup of shredded Mozzarella cheese
- 1/4 tsp. of Cayenne pepper

Directions:

- Just use the 1 1/2 cups of cheddar listed in the ingredients above and follow the recipe for cheese crisps; exclude the Italian spice. If you're using slices of cheese, you should cut each big slice into four squares and bake them. Set alone for cooling.
- Cut the chicken, tomatoes, avocado, and onions into tiny cubes in the meanwhile. Garlic salt, cumin, paprika, and cayenne pepper should all be combined before being added to the mixture of chicken.

- Add tablespoons of the mixture of chicken mixture to the chips after they have cooled for 15 minutes at least and become crispy. Add a few mozzarella cheese slivers to the top of each chip.
- Place into the oven for a few minutes, just long enough for the mozzarella cheese to melt, if desired. The chips will melt if you cook them for too long without checking on them often.

Nutritional values per serving:
Total Calories: 330kcal, **Fat:** 23g, **Carbohydrates:** 4g, **Protein:** 27g

6. Almond Flour Crackers

Ready in: 25 mins.
Serves: 6
Difficulty: easy
Ingredients:

- 1/2 tsp. of Sea salt
- 2 cups of Almond Flour
- 1 Egg, large (beaten)

Directions:

- The oven should be preheated at 350°F (177 degrees C). Use parchment paper to cover a baking sheet.
- In a large bowl, combine the sea salt and almond flour. As the dough develops, add the egg and thoroughly combine
- Between two sizable pieces of parchment paper, sandwich the dough. Roll out the rectangle to a thickness of approximately 1/16 (.2 cm) using a rolling pin
- Create rectangles out of the cracker dough. If desired, prick using a fork or toothpick. Put the baking sheet with the liner. Bake until golden for 8 to 12 minutes.

Nutritional values per serving:
Total Calories: 226kcal, **Fat:** 19g, **Carbohydrates:** 8g, **Protein:** 9g

7. Cauliflower Breadsticks

Ready in: 40 mins.
Serves: 6
Difficulty: easy
Ingredients:

- 1/2 cup of Hemp seeds
- 1 head of Cauliflower
- 2 Eggs (large)
- 3/4 tsp. of Sea salt
- 2 cloves of Garlic (minced)
- 1/4 tsp. of Black pepper
- 1 cup of shredded Mozzarella cheese
- 1 tbsp. of butter, Unsalted (melted)
- Fresh parsley (optional to garnish)

Directions:

- Put the riced cauliflower into a bowl that can go in the microwave for 10 minutes on high in the microwave, or until softened while steaming on the stove. Set alone for cooling.
- In the meanwhile, heat the oven to 425 ° F. (218 degrees C). Use parchment paper to cover a baking sheet.
- The hemp seeds should be processed in a food processor until smooth while cauliflower is cooling.
- Black pepper, sea salt, and eggs are added. Repeat once more until seamless.
- Transfer the cooled cauliflower to a tea towel & press it firmly several

times to extract as much water as you can. Get almost a cup's worth of moisture out.
- Add the riced cauliflower that has been drained to a food processor. Process until uniform.
- Place the "dough" on the baking sheet with parchment paper. About 1/3 inch thick, spread out into a rectangle.
- The top should be firm and begin to turn brown after baking for 13 to 18 minutes.
- Melted butter should be brushed on top. Top with shredded mozzarella and bake for an additional 5 to 10 minutes or till the cheese is melted. The cheese may be browned if desired by placing it under the broiler.
- After somewhat cooled, divide the dough into 24 rectangles the size of breadsticks by cutting it lengthwise in half, then crosswise into 1-inch wide strips.

Nutritional values per serving:
Total Calories: 214kcal, **Fat:** 14g, **Carbohydrates:** 7g, **Protein:** 15g

8. Baked Zucchini Fries

Ready in: 30 mins.
Serves: 4
Difficulty: easy
Ingredients:

- 1 Egg (large)
- 2 Zucchini (medium)
- 3/4 cup of parmesan cheese, Grated
- 1/4 tsp. of Black pepper (optional)
- 1/4 tsp. of Garlic powder

Directions:

- Set the oven up to 425 degrees Fahrenheit (218 degrees C). Bakeware should be lined and gently greased.
- Each zucchini should be divided lengthwise four times. After that, make 16 sticks—each measuring about 4 inches (10 cm) long and 1/2 inch (1 cm) thick—by cutting the sticks once crosswise. If your zucchini sticks seem "wet," use paper towels to pat them dry.
- Two shallow bowls should be ready: one for the beaten egg and the other for the garlic powder, parmesan cheese, and black pepper combination. Each squash stick should be dipped in the egg, shaken off any excess, and then pressed into the mixture of parmesan to coat completely. To prevent getting the excessive egg in the parmesan, which would cause it to clump, use 1 hand for the egg & the other hand for the parmesan. Put in a single layer, touching none of the others, on the prepped baking sheet.
- Fries should be baked until fairly dark brown, approximately 20 minutes, tossing and turning the pan halfway through.
- Put in the broiler for two to three minutes or until crispier and deeper brown.

Nutritional values per serving:
Total Calories: 213kcal, **Fat:** 15g, **Carbohydrates:** 4g, **Protein:** 21g

9. Mozzarella Sticks

Ready in: 20 mins.
Serves: 6
Difficulty: easy
Ingredients:

- 2 tbsp. of Coconut Flour
- 12 pieces of Mozzarella string cheese (in half)
- 1 Egg, large (beaten)
- 1/2 cup of pork rinds, Crushed
- 1/2 cup of Almond Flour
- 2 tsp. of Italian seasoning
- Oil to fry (optional)
- 1/2 tsp. of Garlic powder (optional)

Directions:

- Use parchment paper to cover a cookie sheet. Set aside.
- Fill a small bowl with coconut flour. In a separate small dish, beat the egg. In a third bowl, combine the pork rinds, almond flour, and Italian spice.
- Each slice of mozzarella should be coated with coconut flour. Shake off any excess after dipping it in the egg. Place on the cookie sheet that has been prepared after rolling in the mixture of almond flour thoroughly. Do this with all of the mozzarellas, being careful to keep the pieces apart on the baking pan.
- Until you are ready to bake, place your cookie sheet in the freezer for an hour at least. (Never omit this step! It's essential to do this to stop the cheese from seeping during baking.)

Frying:

- In a skillet, warm 2 tablespoons of oil over medium heat. Fry your mozzarella sticks for 1-2 minutes on each side in a single layer while the oil is heated. When they're golden brown & tender to the touch inside, they are finished.

Baking:

- Set the oven up to 400 degrees Fahrenheit. Place the cookie sheet in the oven after removing it from the freezer (preferably onto the 2nd rack from the lowest). Bake for 5 minutes or until brown on the bottom. Bake for 3–4 more minutes on the opposite side, until brown.

Nutritional values per serving:
Total Calories: 250kcal, **Fat:** 18g, **Carbohydrates:** 5g, **Protein:** 16g

10. Onion Rings

Ready in: 30 mins.
Serves: 6
Difficulty: easy
Ingredients:

- 1 cup of almond flour
- 1 sweet onion (large), cut into rings
- 1 cup of Parmesan cheese, grated
- 1 tsp. of smoked paprika
- 1 tbsp. of baking powder
- Salt & pepper
- 1 tbsp. of heavy cream
- 2 beaten eggs
- cooking spray

Directions:

- Almond flour, baking soda, Parmesan cheese, smoked paprika, salt, &

pepper should all be combined in a medium bowl.

- In another dish, whisk the heavy cream and eggs.
- Onion rings are dipped in eggs, then in a combination of almond flour and salt. Incorporate the onions with the combination of almond flour. Repeat with the rest of the onion, then transfer to a baking sheet lined with parchment paper.
- Air Fryer:
- Your air fryer should be preheated to 350 degrees. Cook the onions in batches as necessary, arranging them in a single layer. (If desired, use air fryer liners to line your air fryer.)
- Cook the onions for 5 minutes after cooking with cooking spray. Carefully turn the onions by reaching underneath with a spatula. Cook for five more minutes and re-spray.
- Baking:
- Set the oven's temperature to 400. Use parchment paper to cover a baking sheet. Spray cooking spray on the onions and arrange them in a single layer. For ten minutes, bake. Turnover and reapply oil. To get crisp and golden, bake for an additional 10 to 12 minutes.

Nutritional values per serving:
Total Calories: 217kcal, **Fat:** 16g, **Carbohydrates:** 7g, **Protein:** 12g

Sides

1. Garlic Bread

Ready in: 45 mins.
Serves: 16
Difficulty: easy
Ingredients:
For bread:

- 6 tbsp. of Unsalted butter
- 1 bag of Bread Mix
- 3/4 cup of almond milk, Unsweetened
- 4 Eggs, large

For garlic bread topping:

- 10 cloves of Garlic (minced)
- 3/4 cup of softened Salted butter (room temperature)
- 2 tbsp. of parmesan cheese, Grated (optional)
- 2 tbsp. of Fresh parsley (chopped)

Directions:

- Set the oven up to 350 degrees Fahrenheit (162 degrees C).
- Use the Bread Mix to make the dough as directed on the container. Use parchment paper to cover a sheet pan before baking rather than a loaf pan. The bread dough should be shaped into a lengthy, rounded loaf that is approximately 13-14 inches (33–35.5 cm) long, 4" (10 cm) was broad, and 1 to 1 & 1/2 inches (2.5–3.8 cm) tall. Put the bread dough on the sheet pan. To vent, make shallow, diagonal incisions at the top.
- 25 minutes should be enough time to bake bread till the top is brown and a toothpick inserted comes out clean. Complete cooling.
- Heat your oven to broil after the bread has cooled.
- Slice your bread loaf into 1.5-inch slices after cutting it in half lengthwise and stacking the two long sections. In all, you should have roughly 16 parts.
- Mash the garlic, butter, and parsley in a medium basin.

- The bread should be covered with garlic butter. If using, top with parmesan cheese.
- On a big baking sheet, arrange your bread in one single layer. For 2-4 minutes in the broiler, till the butter gets melted & the bread's edges are toasted and brown.

Nutritional values per serving:
Total Calories: 266kcal, **Fat:** 23g, **Carbohydrates:** 7g, **Protein:** 9g

2. Bacon Brussels sprouts

Ready in: 40 mins.
Serves: 8
Difficulty: easy
Ingredients:

- 12 strips of Bacon (in half)
- 24 Brussels sprouts, medium (1-inch)
- 1/8 tsp. of Cayenne pepper
- 1/4 cup of Maple Syrup

For the dipping sauce:

- 1 tbsp. of Maple Syrup
- 1/2 cup of Mayonnaise
- 1/2 tbsp. of Dijon mustard
- 1/8 tsp. of Cayenne pepper (to taste)
- 1/2 tsp. of Garlic powder

Directions:

- Set the oven up to 400 degrees Fahrenheit (204 degrees C). Above a baking sheet, place a rack suitable for ovens.
- The halved bacon bits should be spread out in one single layer. Use maple syrup to wipe. Add some cayenne pepper.
- The bottom of the bacon bits should now have maple syrup on them. A bacon slice should be used to encase a Brussels sprout. Put the seam side down on the baking sheet. The remaining sprouts should be repeated. The leftover maple syrup should be drizzled over the bacon and Brussels sprouts.
- Brussels sprouts and bacon should both be cooked for around 25 minutes in the oven.
- Make the sauce in a small dish in the meanwhile. Maple syrup, Mayonnaise, garlic powder, mustard, and cayenne pepper should all be well combined.

Nutritional values per serving:
Total Calories: 267kcal, **Fat:** 24g, **Carbohydrates:** 6g, **Protein:** 6g

3. Italian Stuffed Baked Artichokes with Sausage

Ready in: 1 hr. 15 mins.
Serves: 4
Difficulty: easy
Ingredients:
For artichokes:

- 2 tbsp. of Lemon juice
- 4 Artichokes (large)
- 2 tbsp. of Parmesan cheese, Grated (divided)
- 2 tbsp. of Olive oil

For filling:

- 4 cloves of Garlic (minced)
- 1 lb. of Ground Italian Sausage
- 1/2 cup of Parmesan cheese, Grated (divided)
- 2 tsp. of Italian seasoning

Directions:

- Trim approximately an inch from the tops of artichokes & cut the stems off to produce a flat bottom. Trim the leaves pointed points off using kitchen shears.
- Saltwater in a big saucepan should be brought to a boil. Add the artichokes & keep them immersed in water by placing a heat-safe plate on top of them. 15 minutes of boiling. Remove and place somewhere to drain & cool upside down.
- In the meanwhile, heat your oven to 375°F (190 degrees C).
- Minced garlic, Italian sausage, Italian seasoning, & 1/2 cup grated parmesan should all be mixed immediately before serving in a big bowl. Avoid over-mixing.
- When the artichokes are cooled enough to handle, pat them dry using paper towels before using a spoon to twist apart the center leaves and scrape out the fuzzy choke within. The artichokes should be placed face up in a stoneware baking dish.
- Apply lemon juice & olive oil to the artichokes' tops, sides, and whole body.
- Fill the center and all the spaces between the leaves of each artichoke with the sausage mixture. Add the last two tbsp. (30 grams) of grated parmesan to the artichokes.
- Wrap foil around the baking dish. Bake the sausage for 40–50 minutes, or until it reaches a core temperature of 165°F (74°C), as well as outer leaves are simple to remove.
- Take the foil off. To brown the cheese, preheat oven to broil & lay the filled artichokes underneath the broiler for a few minutes.

Nutritional values per serving:
Total Calories: 604kcal, **Fat:** 47g, **Carbohydrates:** 21g, **Protein:** 28g

4. Garlic Butter Sautéed Mushrooms

Ready in: 20 mins.
Serves: 4
Difficulty: easy
Ingredients:

- 2 tbsp. of Olive oil (divided)
- 1 lb. of sliced Mushrooms (shiitake, cremini, oyster, Portobello, etc.)
- 1/2 tsp. of Sea salt (to taste)
- 2 tbsp. of Unsalted butter
- 1/4 tsp. of Black pepper
- 1/4 cup of reduced sodium Chicken broth
- 2 cloves of Garlic (minced)

Directions:

- Use a moist paper towel to clean the mushrooms. If you'd like, rapidly rinse in a colander; otherwise, pat dry well.
- A tbsp. of olive oil should shimmer and move about the pan readily when tilted after being heated in a big skillet for one to two minutes at medium-high heat.
- Spread out half of mushrooms in one single layer in the pan. Cook

mushrooms for 4-5 minutes, turning once halfway through or until browned and liquid is gone. If mushrooms begin to brown too much, reduce heat to medium.

- Push the mushrooms to the pan's edges after they have browned and shrunk in size to allow for more space in the pan.
- The remaining mushrooms should be arranged in the middle in a single layer with one more tablespoon of oil. Cook the second batch until it is browned and the liquid has evaporated, about 4–5 more minutes, flipping once more halfway through.
- Add salt and pepper to taste and stir the mushrooms.
- Medium-low heat should be used. To create a well and place the butter, push the mushrooms out of the middle of the pan. Add the garlic, then melt it. Sauté until fragrant, for about one minute. Stir in the sautéed mushrooms once garlic has somewhat cooked. Cook the mushrooms for a further 1–2 minutes or until the butter has completely melted.
- Using a wooden spoon, scrape the pan's bottom before adding the broth. Raise the heat to a simmer, & then cook for an additional two to three minutes or until the liquid either evaporates completely or is absorbed by the mushrooms.

Nutritional values per serving:
Total Calories: 141kcal, **Fat:** 13g, **Carbohydrates:** 4g, **Protein:** 3g

5. Asparagus Casserole

Ready in: 20 mins.
Serves: 8
Difficulty: easy
Ingredients:
For casserole:

- 2 tbsp. of Olive oil
- 2 lbs. of Asparagus (trimmed)
- 4 cloves of Garlic (minced)
- 1/4 tsp. of Black pepper
- 1/4 tsp. of Sea salt
- 1 1/4 cups of shredded Mozzarella cheese
- 1 1/4 cups of shredded Cheddar cheese

For topping:

- 2 tbsp. of chopped Chives
- 3/4 cup of Hollandaise sauce

Directions:

- Set the oven up to 400 degrees Fahrenheit (204 degrees C).
- In a baking dish about 7 by 10 inches, put the asparagus.
- Arrange asparagus in a big bowl and toss it with olive oil, salt, garlic, and pepper. To coat everything evenly, shuffle the pieces.
- The baking dish should be filled with 1/3 of asparagus and topped with 1/3 of cheese. For a sum of three layers of each, repeat.
- Bake asparagus for 15 to 20 minutes, depending on how done you want it.
- Make the sauce in the meanwhile using these directions.
- Sprinkle chopped chives on top and pour hollandaise over the finished asparagus.

Nutritional values per serving:
Total Calories: 256kcal, **Fat:** 22g, **Carbohydrates:** 3g, **Protein:** 11g

6. Okra

Ready in: 15 mins.
Serves: 4
Difficulty: easy
Ingredients:

- 1 lb. of Okra (frozen or fresh, sliced in 1" thick circles)
- Cooking spray
- 1 tbsp. of Olive oil
- 1 tsp. of Paprika
- 1 tsp. of Garlic powder
- 1/4 tsp. of Cayenne pepper
- 1 tsp. of Sea salt

Directions:

- Spray cooking oil on the air fryer basket.
- Set the air fryer up to 350 degrees Fahrenheit (176 degrees C).
- Okra, garlic powder, olive oil, paprika, sea salt, & cayenne pepper should all be combined in a medium bowl. Blend to coat. (There is no need to defrost frozen okra.)
- Okra should be arranged in a single layer into the air fryer basket. Avoid crowding since air circulation is essential for the greatest effects. Based on the size of the air fryer, you might have to do it in 3-4 batches.
- Fresh: Fry fresh okra into the air fryer for 8-10 minutes, stirring halfway through.
- Frozen: In the air fryer, cook frozen okra for 15 minutes, stirring once.

Nutritional values per serving:
Total Calories: 72kcal, **Fat:** 4g, **Carbohydrates:** 9g, **Protein:** 2g

7. Cabbage Steaks

Ready in: 50 mins.
Serves: 8
Difficulty: easy
Ingredients:

- 1 head of Cabbage
- 8 slices of Bacon
- 8 cloves of Garlic (minced)
- 2 tbsp. of Lemon juice
- 1/4 cup of Olive oil
- 1/2 tsp. of Black pepper
- 1/2 tsp. of Sea salt

Directions:

- Put the bacon pieces in a large, chilly pan. Set the heat to medium-low and place it on the stove. Flipping the bacon as necessary, fry for 8 to 10 minutes or until crispy.
- Slice the cabbage in 3/4-inch thick pieces in the meanwhile.
- Combine the lemon juice, olive oil, sea salt, & black pepper in a big resealable plastic bag.
- The bacon grease remains in the pan after you remove the bacon and put it aside to drain. For approximately a minute, until aromatic, add the minced garlic.
- Let the fat bacon pan cool for five to ten minutes. Pour the bacon grease and sautéed garlic into a plastic bag after it has cooled enough not to melt the plastic. Add any extra garlic by scooping it with a spatula. For the marinade, seal and thoroughly combine.
- Sliced cabbage steaks should be added to the marinating bag. Apply a good coating. For at least 28-30 minutes, refrigerate.
- Grill over medium heat for preheating.
- Cook cabbage steaks for 4 to 8 mins on each side, turning once until they are crisp and tender throughout.
- Serve with cooked bacon & garnished with parsley (optional).

Nutritional values per serving:
Total Calories: 184kcal, **Fat:** 15g, **Carbohydrates:** 8g, **Protein:** 4g

8. Spicy Lupini Beans

Ready in: 20 mins.
Serves: 6
Difficulty: easy
Ingredients:

- 1 tbsp. of Lime juice
- 1 1/2 cups of Lupini beans (jarred, canned, or vacuum sealed)
- 1 tbsp. of Olive oil
- 1/4 tsp. of Sea salt
- 1 tsp. of Chili powder
- 1/4 tsp. of Black pepper

Directions:

- Lupini beans should be drained. In a colander, rinse, and then pat dry.
- Mix the lime juice, chili powder, olive oil, sea salt, & black pepper in a medium bowl. Lupini beans should be added and coated.
- Lupini beans should be placed in the base of the basket of air fryer to cook in the machine. 10 minutes of air frying at 380 degrees Fahrenheit (193 degrees Celsius), stirring halfway through.
- Lupini beans should be arranged onto a baking sheet in one single layer to cook in the oven. 15 minutes of baking at 400 °F (204 degrees C), tossing halfway through.

Nutritional values per serving:
Total Calories: 61kcal, **Fat:** 3g, **Carbohydrates:** 3g, **Protein:** 4g

9. Eggplant

Ready in: 15 mins.
Serves: 4
Difficulty: easy

Ingredients:

- 2 tbsp. of Olive oil
- 1 Eggplant, medium (sliced)
- 1 tsp. of Sea salt
- 1 cup of parmesan cheese, Grated
- 1/2 tsp. of Black pepper
- 2 tsp. of Italian seasoning

Directions:

- Set the air fryer up to 375°F before using it (190 degrees C).
- Cut circles out of the eggplant that is approximately half an inch thick. Just remove the leafy end after you have finished slicing so that you have more to hold onto.
- Olive oil should be drizzled or brushed over the eggplant pieces. Add Italian spice, Parmesan cheese, sea salt, and black pepper.
- Put a single layer of eggplant slices in the basket of an air fryer. Sauté the eggplant for 10 to 12 minutes, or until it is tender, & the cheese is browned. Using the remaining eggplant slices, repeat in batches.

Nutritional values per serving:
Total Calories: 202kcal, **Fat:** 14g, **Carbohydrates:** 8g, **Protein:** 10g

10. Roasted Garlic Bok Choy

Ready in: 30 mins.
Serves: 4
Difficulty: easy
Ingredients:

- 1/4 cup of Avocado oil
- 1 large head of Bok Choy
- 1 tsp. of Sea salt
- 4 cloves of Garlic (minced)
- 1/2 tsp. of Black pepper

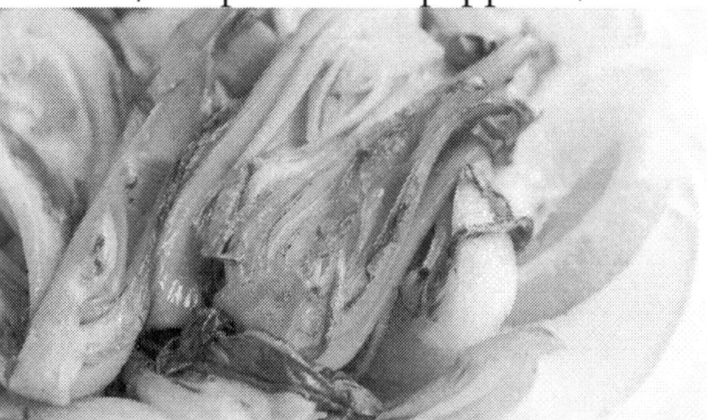

Directions:

- Set the oven up to 425 degrees Fahrenheit (218 degrees C).
- Based on how thick & leafy it is, cut the bok Choy in fourths or eighths lengthwise.
- Place the bok Choy cut side down in one single layer onto a large baking sheet. Add two tablespoons of avocado oil. Put half of the salt & pepper on top. On the other side, repeat the oil, salt, and pepper.
- Invert one more so that the cut side is facing up. Using your hands, cover Bok Choy with minced garlic.
- On the bottom shelf of the oven, roast your bok Choy for 10 minutes. Flip the pan and continue roasting for an additional 10 minutes or until the leaves begin to brown gently.

Nutritional values per serving:
Total Calories: 153kcal, **Fat:** 14g, **Carbohydrates:** 5g, **Protein:** 3g

CHAPTER 6:
Keto Diet - Soup, Stews and Salads Recipes
Soups & Stews

1. Chicken Fajita Soup

Ready in: 3 hrs. 20 mins.
Serves: 8
Difficulty: medium
Ingredients:

- 1 cup of chicken broth
- 2 lbs. of skinless, boneless chicken breasts
- 1 chopped onion
- 3 cloves of garlic minced
- 1 chopped green pepper
- 1 tbsp. of butter
- 2 cans of tomatoes (diced) with green chillis (10 oz.)
- 6 oz. of cream cheese
- 2½ cups of chicken broth
- 2½ tbsp. of homemade taco seasoning
- ½ cup of heavy whipping cream
- salt & pepper to taste

Directions:

- Cook skinless & boneless chicken breasts in a cup of chicken stock in a slow cooker for 2-3 hours on high or 5-6 hours on low. Pepper and salt to taste.
- Remove the chicken from the slow cooker after it is fully cooked, then shred it. (You may drain the soup's remaining stock.)
- Green pepper, onion, & garlic are sautéed in 1 tbsp. of butter until transparent in a big pot.
- Mash the cream cheese into the vegetables with a spoon to get a homogeneous mixture as it melts.
- Add the tinned tomatoes, chicken stock, heavy whipping cream, & taco seasoning.
- For 20 minutes, simmer on low with the lid off.
- Cover the pot and boil for 10 minutes after adding the chicken shreds.
- To taste, add salt and pepper.
- Cilantro, Shredded cheese, avocado, green onions, and/or sour cream are optional additions to each dish.

Nutritional values per serving:
Total Calories: 306kcal, **Fat:** 17g, **Carbohydrates:** 8g, **Protein:** 26g

2. Zuppa Toscana Soup

Ready in: 30 mins.
Serves: 8
Difficulty: easy
Ingredients:

- 3 slices of bacon, sliced in smaller bits
- 1 pound of sausage (ground)
- 1 cup of chopped onion
- 1 head of cauliflower (fresh), chopped
- 3 cloves of garlic, chopped
- 5 cups of chicken broth, low-sodium
- salt & pepper to taste
- 1 tsp. of dried oregano
- 1 cup of whipping cream (heavy)
- Parmesan, to top (optional)
- 3 cups of kale (fresh), stems removed

Directions:

- Over medium-high heat, add the slices of bacon & sausage to a large saucepan (a Dutch oven works best).
- Fry the bacon and sausage until they are well-browned. While keeping a few tablespoons of the fat in the saucepan for flavor, drain any extra fat. (I did not need to remove any fat.)
- When the onions are transparent, add the chopped onion & simmer for a further two to three minutes.
- Add the oregano, fresh cauliflower, garlic, and chicken broth. To blend, stir.
- Medium heat should be used with the pot covered. Sauté the cauliflower for 15 minutes or until it is tender and easily punctured with a fork.
- Remove the lid from the saucepan, then add the chopped kale, heavy cream, and salt & pepper to taste.
- The kale needs to cook for a few minutes until it wilts.
- Before serving, let cool.

Nutritional values per serving:
Total Calories: 309kcal, **Fat:** 24g, **Carbohydrates:** 5g, **Protein:** 12g

3. Broccoli Cheddar Soup

Ready in: 35 mins.
Serves: 6
Difficulty: easy
Ingredients:

- 3 cups of cheddar cheese, shredded
- 4 cups of broccoli florets, chopped
- 2 cups of whipping cream, heavy
- 1.5 cups of onions, diced (half onion)
- 2 cups of broth or water
- 1 cup of carrots, diced (3 carrots)
- 2 tbsp. of salted butter
- 1 cup of celery, diced (3 stalks)
- 5 strips of bacon
- salt & pepper, to taste
- 5 cloves of garlic, minced

Directions:

- For cooking bacon, arrange the strips in a single layer in a big saucepan and heat it to medium. Cook for 5 to 10 minutes, flipping regularly or until crispy. Place the bacon on a dish covered with paper towels to drain.

- Add chopped celery, onions, and carrots to the saucepan with the bacon drippings to sauté. Cook for approximately 10 minutes, stirring regularly, over medium heat, till softened.
- Broccoli should be cooked in a saucepan with water, heavy whipping cream, plus broccoli. Simmer on a medium-high heat setting. Stir regularly and lower heat as necessary to continue simmering while you cook the broccoli uncovered for 5 to 10 minutes.
- Cheddar cheese should be gradually added and stirred into the soup until melted. Stir in the butter & minced garlic after adding them.
- Cook soup for approximately 10 minutes or until desired consistency is reached, then serve. Add salt & pepper to taste after letting the soup cool down a little. Serve in dishes and sprinkle with crumbled bacon.

Nutritional values per serving:
Total Calories: 490kcal, **Fat:** 45g, **Carbohydrates:** 13g, **Protein:** 13g

4. Beef Stew

Ready in: 1 hr. 30 mins.
Serves: 6
Difficulty: easy
Ingredients:

- 1/2 tsp. of Sea salt
- 2 lb. of stew meat (cut in 1" pieces)
- 1/4 tsp. of Black pepper
- 1 Onion, medium (diced)
- 2 tbsp. of Olive oil (divided)
- 2 Carrots, medium (peeled & sliced into ¼" thick circles)
- 1 tsp. of Italian seasoning
- 2 cloves of Garlic (minced)
- 1 lb. of Celery root (with peel & stems)
- 1 can of Diced tomatoes (14.5-oz.)
- 6 cups of Beef bone broth
- 2 Bay leaves, medium

Directions:

- Add salt and pepper to the steak to season it. (Since the broth would be salty, it will only be a light quantity.)
- In a big Dutch oven, heat a tbsp of oil over medium heat. One layer of meat should be added. (If you cannot get the meat on the base of the pan in a single layer, work in batches.) Each batch should be seared for 8 to 10 minutes total, moving only after every side has thoroughly browned. The steak should be taken out and placed on a platter.
- The same Dutch oven is used to heat a further tablespoon of oil. Include the carrots and onions. Sauté till tender and just beginning to brown, approximately 10 minutes.
- Italian spice and garlic are added. Sauté until aromatic for approximately a minute.
- Reintroduce the meat in the Dutch oven. Add the full bay leaves, diced tomatoes, and broth. Remove any browned residue from the pot's bottom by scraping.

- When the meat is tender, turn down the heat to medium- to low, cover the pot, & simmer for 45 to 60 minutes.
- The celery root should be added. To bring it back to a boil, turn up the heat. When soft, cover & simmer for 15 minutes.
- Take away the bay leaves. If necessary, taste and adjust the salt and pepper.

Nutritional values per serving:
Total Calories: 410kcal, **Fat:** 22g, **Carbohydrates:** 14g, **Protein:** 36g

5. Chicken Soup & Cauliflower Rice

Ready in: 30 mins.
Serves: 4
Difficulty: easy
Ingredients:

- 2 stalks of celery, chopped
- 2 tbsp. of avocado oil
- 1/4 cup of chopped onions
- 2 cloves of garlic, minced
- salt & pepper, to taste
- 1/2 tsp. of thyme leaves, dried
- 4 cups of chicken broth
- 1/2 tsp. of paprika
- 8 ounces of riced cauliflower (2 cups)
- 1 pound of skinless & boneless chicken thighs, cubed

Directions:

- In a big saucepan set over medium heat, warm the oil. Salt and pepper the celery & onions before adding them. Sauté the veggies for approximately 5 minutes, stirring regularly, until they are soft.
- After approximately a minute, add the thyme, garlic, and paprika & simmer until fragrant. Bring to a boil while stirring in the broth.
- Simmer the mixture while adding the chicken and cauliflower that have been riced. Simmer for 12 minutes or until the cauliflower is soft and the chicken is well-cooked. To taste, add more or less salt and pepper.

Nutritional values per serving:
Total Calories: 196kcal, **Fat:** 5g, **Carbohydrates:** 10g, **Protein:** 26g

6. Broccoli Chicken Cheese Bacon Soup

Ready in: 25 mins.
Serves: 8
Difficulty: easy
Ingredients:

- two tbsp. of butter

- 1 cup of rotisserie or cooked chicken, shredded
- ⅓ a yellow diced onion
- 2 cloves of minced garlic
- 2 ribs of celery diced
- two cups of chicken broth
- 4 cups of florets of broccoli, chopped
- 1 ⅔ cups of heavy cream
- 3 cups of cheddar cheese, shredded
- 3 ounces of softened cream cheese, cubed
- ½ cup of jack cheese, shredded
- ½ tsp. of nutmeg
- 1 tsp. of black pepper, freshly ground
- ¼ tsp. of sea salt
- ½ tsp. of xanthan gum (optional)
- 4 slices of bacon (cooked), crumbled

Directions:

- When using the Instant Pot, choose Sauté (Normal). Add butter and let it melt in the heated Instant Pot.
- Add the onions, celery, & garlic after the butter has melted. Continually whisk for 5 minutes or until softened veggies and transparent onions are.
- When the fluid in the saucepan begins to boil, switch off your Instant Pot and add the chicken broth & broccoli florets.
- Turn the steam escape handle towards the Sealing position, close the lid, and cover.
- Set the timer to cook for 5 minutes and choose the Pressure Cook on High Pressure.
- After the cooking is finished, remove the remaining pressure quickly after allowing the pressure to naturally release for 10-15 minutes (do nothing during that time).
- The cream cheese, sea salt, nutmeg, and black pepper are added after you remove the Instant Pot's cover. To blend, stir. Stir in the chicken that has been shredded.
- Choose Sauté (Normal) and wait for the soup to begin boiling. Shredded Cheddar & Jack cheeses should be added gradually while stirring constantly.
- Choose the Keep Warm option on the Instant Pot after the cheese has melted. Cream heavy is added; whisk.
- Add xanthan gum powder into the saucepan and stir until thickened, if required, to thicken.
- Serve the soup hot, and ladle 1/2 spoonful of the cooked & crumbled bacon into each bowl.

Nutritional values per serving:
Total Calories: 377kcal, **Fat:** 28g, **Carbohydrates:** 5g, **Protein:** 23g

7. Cabbage Beef Soup

Ready in: 40 mins.
Serves: 8
Difficulty: easy
Ingredients:

- 1 chopped yellow Onion
- 1 lb. of ground beef
- 2 chopped celery ribs

- 1 seeded Green Bell Pepper, chopped
- 1 chopped carrot
- 3 cloves of garlic, grated or minced
- 1 tbsp. of Italian Seasoning, Dried
- 1 tbsp. of Spicy Brown Mustard
- 1 tsp. of Smoked Paprika
- 28 ounces of Crushed Tomatoes, Fire Roasted
- 32 ounces of Beef Broth
- 2 Sprigs of Fresh Thyme
- 1 Green Cabbage, chopped (core removed)
- Salt & black Pepper, to taste

Directions:

- Brown the ground meat in an enormous soup saucepan. Drain any extra fat from the saucepan and set aside (leaving about 2-3 Tb).
- Sauté onion, celery, carrot, and green pepper in oil over medium-high heat. If necessary, add extra oil.
- When the veggies are ready, add the garlic and sauté for 1 minute.
- Bring back the ground beef to the saucepan and season with Italian seasoning, brown mustard, and smoked paprika. Stir.
- Tomato sauce, beef broth, and thyme should be added. Stirring often, bring to a boil, then simmer for 15 to 20 minutes.
- Add the cabbage, then cook it until it is soft (10-15 minutes). To taste, add salt and pepper. If additional liquid is needed, add more water or broth.
- Serve on its own or with rice.

Nutritional values per serving:
Total Calories: 190kcal, **Fat:** 10g, **Carbohydrates:** 6g, **Protein:** 18g

8. Creamy Taco Ground Beef Soup

Ready in: 30 mins.
Serves: 8
Difficulty: easy
Ingredients:

- ½ cup of chopped onion
- 1 pound of ground beef
- 2 cloves of garlic, minced
- 1 tsp. of chili powder
- 1 tbsp. of ground cumin
- 1 package of cream cheese (8 ounces), softened
- 2 cans of diced tomatoes & green chiles (10 ounces)
- 2 cans of beef broth (14.5 ounces)
- 2 tsp. of salt
- ½ cup of heavy cream

Directions:

- Over medium-high heat, combine ground beef, onion, & garlic in a big soup pot. Sauté and stir the meat for 5 to 7 minutes, or until it is browned and crumbly. Drain and get rid of oil. Cook 2 minutes longer before adding cumin and chili powder.
- With a large spoon, mash the cream cheese into meat in the saucepan until there are no longer any white spots, about 3 to 5 minutes. Add salt, heavy cream, chopped tomatoes, and broth. Cook for a further 10 minutes or until well heated.

Nutritional values per serving:
Total Calories: 288kcal, **Fat:** 24g, **Carbohydrates:** 5g, **Protein:** 13g

9. Creamy Turkey Soup with Kale and Cabbage

Ready in: 50 mins.
Serves: 8
Difficulty: easy
Ingredients:

- 1 onion (small), chopped
- 2 tbsp. of coconut oil
- 2 ribs of celery
- 13.5 ounces of coconut milk
- 3 cloves of garlic, minced
- 1 ½ cups of radishes, chopped
- 1 quart of turkey broth
- 2 cups of turkey, cooked & cubed
- 3 sprigs of thyme leaves, fresh
- ⅛ tsp. of black pepper, ground
- 1 tsp. of sea salt
- 5 ounces of roughly chopped kale
- 8 ounces of cabbage, thinly sliced

Directions:

- Melt coconut oil in a Dutch oven or big saucepan over high heat. Sauté onions & celery in heated oil till onions are transparent. Throw in garlic and sauté until fragrant.
- Coconut milk should be added and heated until totally liquefied. Combine turkey and radishes. Add the turkey broth.
- Add thyme, salt, & pepper for seasoning. Next, cover & simmer for 15 mins after bringing it to a boil.
- Open the top and add the kale and cabbage. Cook for a further five minutes while covered.

Nutritional values per serving:
Total Calories: 191kcal, **Fat:** 15g, **Carbohydrates:** 7g, **Protein:** 8g

10. Tomato Soup

Ready in: 25 mins.
Serves: 6
Difficulty: easy
Ingredients:

- ⅔ cup of heavy whipping cream
- 24 ounces of marinara sauce, low-carb
- ½ cup of chicken broth
- 1 tsp. of Italian seasoning
- 1 tbsp. of tomato paste
- salt & black pepper to taste

Garnish (optional):

- Parsley
- Bacon, crumbled

Directions:

- Put a saucepan on the stovetop over medium heat and add the marinara sauce.
- Add the tomato paste, Italian seasoning, chicken broth, and salt and pepper to taste. Mix well by stirring.
- The mixture should just barely begin to boil.
- Turn the heat down to medium or low, stir the heavy whipping cream in, and simmer for 8-10 minutes.
- Serve topped with parsley & crumbled bacon if preferred.

Nutritional values per serving:
Total Calories: 121kcal, **Fat:** 10g, **Carbohydrates:** 8g, **Protein:** 2g

11. Egg Drop Soup

Ready in: 35 mins.
Serves: 4
Difficulty: easy
Ingredients:

- 1 tsp. of Ginger paste
- 4 cups of Chicken broth
- 8 ounces of sliced mushrooms
- ⅓ cup of green onions, Chopped
- 1 tbsp. of Soy sauce
- Salt & white pepper, as per taste
- 3 large Eggs, lightly beaten

Directions:

- In a saucepan over medium-high heat on the stove, combine the chicken broth, mushrooms, ginger paste, soy sauce, green onions, and salt & white pepper to taste.
- The mixture should boil before being simmered for 15 minutes.
- Stirring while carefully incorporating the eggs.
- Before serving, simmer for a few more minutes.

Nutritional values per serving:
Total Calories: 84kcal, **Fat:** 4g, **Carbohydrates:** 4g, **Protein:** 8g

12. French Onion Soup

Ready in: 1 hr. 5 mins.
Serves: 6
Difficulty: easy
Ingredients:

- 4 tbsp. of butter
- 2 onions (medium), sliced
- 3 tsp. of brown sugar substitute
- 6 cups of beef broth
- ¼ tsp. of xanthan gum
- ¼ cup of white cooking wine
- 1 tsp. of fresh thyme, chopped
- 1 tsp. of Worcestershire sauce
- 2 bay leaves
- 1 tbsp. of butter melted
- 1 batch of 90-second bread
- ½ tsp. of garlic powder
- Parsley (chopped) for garnish
- 1 cup of gruyere cheese, grated

Directions:

- Over medium heat, add the onions and 4 tbsp. Butter to the pan. Sauté until softened & caramelized for 15 to 20 minutes.
- Sauté while incorporating white cooking wine till the liquid is cut in half.
- Add the beef broth, fresh thyme, Worcestershire sauce, and bay leaves in addition to the brown sugar replacement. Spend 15 minutes simmering.
- Slice one batch of 90-second bread into cubes after preparation. On a baking sheet with parchment paper, arrange the cubes & broil them till browned.
- Garlic powder is added after the melted butter is brushed over the bread pieces.
- Add the xanthan gum to the soup, then cook it for a while to thicken it.
- Sliced gruyere cheese, toasted bread cubes, and chopped parsley are served as garnish.

Nutritional values per serving:
Total Calories: 257kcal, **Fat:** 20g, **Carbohydrates:** 6g, **Protein:** 12g

13. Cream of the Asparagus Soup

Ready in: 35 mins.
Serves: 5
Difficulty: easy
Ingredients:

- 2 tbsp. of Butter, unsalted
- 2 pounds of Asparagus spears, chopped in 1" pieces, ends removed
- ½ chopped Onion
- 3 cups of Chicken broth
- 3 tsp. of Minced garlic
- 1 cup of Heavy whipping cream
- Fresh chives (chopped) for garnish
- Salt & pepper to taste

Directions:

- On a stovetop over medium heat, melt the butter.
- The onions should be added to the stew and sautéed until tender.
- The asparagus bits should start to become a little soft when you stir them in.
- Garlic, salt, & pepper, to taste, should all be combined. Stir-fry for 30 more seconds.
- After adding the chicken broth, boil the mixture for 10 to 15 minutes.
- After allowing it to cool for a little while, transfer the mixture of soup to a food processor or blender.
- The soup should be well-smoothed.
- Add extra salt & pepper to taste, heavy whipping cream, and the soup mixture back to the pot.
- After 5 more minutes of simmering, garnish with chopped chives and serve.

Nutritional values per serving:
Total Calories: 258kcal, **Fat:** 23g, **Carbohydrates:** 11g, **Protein:** 6g

14. Thai Coconut Soup

Ready in: 35 mins.
Serves: 5
Difficulty: easy
Ingredients:

- 1 tbsp. of Ginger paste
- 1 tbsp. of Olive oil
- 1 tsp. of red Thai curry paste
- 3 cups of Chicken broth
- 2 tbsp. of Fish sauce
- 1 Can of Coconut milk
- 8 ounces of sliced mushrooms
- 1 tbsp. of brown sugar
- ½ Medium chopped onion
- 1 tbsp. of Lime juice
- 2-3 cups of Shredded chicken
- Chopped cilantro for garnish
- Salt to taste

Directions:

- Heat olive oil in a saucepan or deep-sided pan over medium heat.
- Curry paste and ginger paste should be added to the oil & cooked until aromatic.

- After the brown sugar substitute has melted, blend it with the fish sauce.
- Add the coconut milk and chicken broth. Heat till a low boil is reached.
- The mushrooms & onions are added after lowering the heat to simmer. Boil the veggies until they are tender.
- After adding the lime juice and chicken shreds, simmer for an extra 5 minutes.
- Before serving, season with salt to taste & add chopped cilantro as a garnish.

Nutritional values per serving:
Total Calories: 366kcal, **Fat:** 27g, **Carbohydrates:** 6g, **Protein:** 28g

15. Ratatouille Italian Sausage Stew

Ready in: 1 hr. 50 mins.
Serves: 6
Difficulty: easy
Ingredients:

- 3 tbsp. of olive oil
- 1 package of turkey Italian sausage, uncooked (19.5 oz.)
- 2 chopped zucchini, medium
- 1/2 chopped red onion, small
- 2 chopped yellow summer squash, medium
- 2 tbsp. of minced garlic
- 1 chopped yellow pepper, medium
- 6 yellow or red tomatoes, medium (chopped)
- 1 chopped red pepper, medium
- 1 tsp. of dried oregano
- 3 tbsp. of fresh parsley, chopped
- 1/2 cup of sliced or chopped fresh basil, plus some more for garnishing
- salt & pepper to taste

Directions:

- Italian sausage should be cooked until it is browned across all sides in a little quantity of hot olive oil in a big, heavy pan.
- Sausage should be placed onto a cutting board to cool.
- Next, after adding a little more oil, sauté the zucchini & yellow squash for approximately 5 minutes or until it begins to turn a light brown.
- Squash may be taken out of the pan and put aside.
- More olive oil should be added, after which onions, peppers, and garlic should be cooked for 3–4 minutes.
- Add tomatoes to the skillet, toss the veggies together gently, reduce heat to medium, and simmer for an additional 5 minutes.
- Re-add the yellow squash and zucchini to the pan along with the salt, pepper, dried oregano, and parsley.
- Cook uncovered for around 30 minutes on low heat. (If you'd like, you may add some more olive oil.)
- Cut the sausage diagonally in slices & add to the skillet and cook for 30-45 minutes longer.
- After the sausage is well cooked and the stew is delicious, add fresh basil, slice it or chop it, season with sea salt, and simmer for an additional 5 to 10 minutes.
- Serve hot or at room temperature, and if preferred, top with additional

sliced basil & Parmesan cheese when guests arrive.

- This reheats easily and keeps for many days in the refrigerator.

Nutritional values per serving:
Total Calories: 325kcal, **Fat:** 18g, **Carbohydrates:** 16g, **Protein:** 27g

16. Chicken Stew

Ready in: 45 mins.
Serves: 4
Difficulty: easy
Ingredients:

- 1/4 cup of red onion, finely diced
- 2 tbsp. of olive oil
- 1 tbsp. of ginger root, finely minced
- Salt, to taste
- 2 tsp. of jalapeno, finely minced
- 1 tsp. of chile powder
- 1/2 cup of natural peanut butter, chunky
- 1 cup of chicken stock
- 2 tbsp. of tomato paste
- 3 cups of cooked diced chicken
- 1 tbsp. of cider vinegar
- 2 thinly sliced green onions
- and black pepper, freshly ground to taste

Directions:

- Chop the chicken coarsely, along with the ginger, red onion, and jalapeño.
- Ginger, Onion, and jalapenos should be finely chopped. Heat oil in a heavy skillet. Add the ingredients, season with salt, & cook for 2 minutes. Add the chile powder, combine it with the other ingredients, and cook for an additional minute. Add tomato paste, apple cider vinegar, peanut butter, chicken stock, and peanut butter and whisk while bringing to a gentle boil.
- As it begins to boil, turn down the heat to a very low simmer, add the chicken, gently mix to blend and simmer for 10 to 15 minutes. (Resist the impulse to stir it too much; doing so may cause the chicken to fall apart, which is not what you want.)
- Green onions may be washed, dried, and cut while the mixture simmers. If the peanut butter oil has separated after 10 to 15 minutes, gently whisk it again. Serve hot, garnishing each portion with a copious amount of green onion slices.

Nutritional values per serving:
Total Calories: 524kcal, **Fat:** 38g, **Carbohydrates:** 9g, **Protein:** 35g

17. Pork Green Chile Stew

Ready in: 1 hr. 45 mins.
Serves: 8
Difficulty: easy

Ingredients:

- 2 tsp. of ground cumin
- 2 pounds of pork loin (cubed)
- 2 tsp. of granulated garlic
- 2 ounces of onion (about a half cup, chopped)
- 1 tsp. of ground pure chile powder, optional
- 2 cloves of garlic
- 3 tbsp. of oil
- 1 can of Hatch green chilies & liquid, whole (27-ounce can)
- poached or fried eggs, optional
- 2 cups of water

Directions:

- Pork loin slices are browned in hot oil in a large frying pan.
- Chop the garlic and onion in the meanwhile. Open a can of chilies & pulse them in a blender with the garlic and onion until they resemble a thick, chunky mixture. Stir the spices into the cooked pork until they are aromatic. Over the browned pork, add the pureed chilies and their liquid from the can.
- Pour the can of liquid along with the 2 cups of water. Wait till the very last minute before adding any salt. Stir and lower heat to medium-low or low. The pork should be tender after simmering for 1 to 1 1/2 hours with the cover slightly ajar on the pan. The stew made with green chiles won't taste well without adding chicken stock, which will make it overly salty. It will be highly tasty merely by adding water.
- Seasonings should be adjusted. Pour into a bowl over the zoodles and cauliflower rice, and then top with a poached or fried egg (optional).

Nutritional values per serving:
Total Calories: 182kcal, **Fat:** 10g, **Carbohydrates:** 4g, **Protein:** 20g

18. Brazilian Shrimp Stew

Ready in: 25 mins.
Serves: 6
Difficulty: easy
Ingredients:

- 1/4 cup of olive oil
- 1 1/2 lbs. of peeled raw shrimp, deveined
- 1/4 cup of onion, diced
- 1/4 cup of red pepper (roasted), diced
- 1 clove of garlic, minced
- 1 can of diced tomatoes (14 oz.)
- 2 tbsp. of Sriracha hot sauce
- 1 cup of coconut milk
- 2 tbsp. of fresh lime juice
- salt & pepper to taste
- 1/4 cup of chopped fresh cilantro

Directions:

- In a small saucepan, heat the olive oil.
- After cooking the onions until they are transparent for a few minutes, add the garlic & roasted peppers and simmer for an additional few minutes.
- To the pan, add the shrimp, tomatoes, and cilantro. Gently boil for 3 minutes or until the shrimp becomes opaque.

- Add the coconut milk & Sriracha sauce, & heat them up briefly without boiling.
- Add the lime juice, then taste and adjust the salt and pepper.
- Serve hot with fresh cilantro as a garnish.

Nutritional values per serving:
Total Calories: 294kcal, **Fat:** 19g, **Carbohydrates:** 5g, **Protein:** 24g

19. Lamb Stew

Ready in: 3 hr. 5 mins.
Serves: 4
Difficulty: easy
Ingredients:

- 8 oz. of turnips, peeled & chopped
- 1 lb. of lamb stewing meat, boneless
- 8 oz. of sliced mushrooms, quartered
- 1 tsp. of onion powder
- 14 oz. can beef broth
- 1 tsp. of garlic paste
- pinch of xanthan gum, optional
- salt & pepper
- chopped fresh parsley (flat-leaf) to garnish

Directions:

- Sliced or quartered mushrooms, cooked turnip, and lamb should all be added to a slow cooker dish or Instant Pot.
- Add salt, pepper, garlic paste, onion powder, and beef broth next. Stir well.
- Cook for three hours on high heat or six hours on low heat.
- If necessary, recheck the seasoning and add more. Transfer the lamb & veggies to a serving plate using a slotted spoon, then drizzle some sauce on top. Note: After removing the lamb and vegetables, mix in a sprinkle of xanthan gum if you like a little thicker liquid.
- Add freshly cut flat-leaf parsley as a garnish.

Nutritional values per serving:
Total Calories: 190kcal, **Fat:** 6g, **Carbohydrates:** 6g, **Protein:** 27g

20. Chicken Cacciatore Stew

Ready in: 30 mins.
Serves: 6
Difficulty: easy
Ingredients:

- 1 diced Onion

- 3 tbsp. of avocado oil
- 1 diced Red bell pepper
- 6 skinless Boneless chicken thighs in 1" pieces
- 3 Cloves of garlic, minced
- 1 Can of diced tomatoes (28 ounces) with juice
- 1 ½ tsp. of Dried oregano
- 3 tbsp. of Drained capers
- Kosher salt & pepper to taste
- ¼ Cup of fresh basil leaves, Chopped

Directions:

- In a Dutch oven with a thick bottom, heat avocado oil on medium heat. Add the minced garlic, bell pepper, and onion. It takes roughly 8 minutes to sauté softly.
- Chicken diced should be added after seasoning with salt and pepper. Cook until chicken is cooked on both sides. Tomatoes, oregano, capers, and basil should be added. Once the chicken is fully cooked, simmer uncovered. 15 to 20 minutes.
- To taste, add salt & pepper to the food. Serve with spaghetti squash, zucchini noodles, or a side salad.

Nutritional values per serving:
Total Calories: 355kcal, **Fat:** 20g, **Carbohydrates:** 10g, **Protein:** 39g

Salads

1. Cobb Salad

Ready in: 10 mins.
Serves: 8
Difficulty: easy
Ingredients:

- 5 cups of chopped Watercress
- 5 cups of chopped Romaine lettuce
- 8 slices of cooked bacon, crumbled (or in small pieces)
- 2 cups of halved Grape tomatoes
- 12 oz. of chicken breast, cooked (cut in cubes or can be shredded)
- 2 Avocados (medium)
- 1/2 cup of crumbled Roquefort cheese
- 4 hard-boiled eggs, large (sliced or diced)
- 2 tbsp. of finely chopped chives
- Sea salt (as per taste)
- 1/2 cup of Ranch dressing
- Black pepper (as per taste)

Directions:

- Combine all the ingredients in a big bowl except the dressing, salt, and pepper.
- Mix in the dressing before adding it. Use salt and pepper to taste to season.

Nutritional values per serving:
Total Calories: 374kcal, **Fat:** 27g, **Carbohydrates:** 8g, **Protein:** 24g

2. Beef Salad

Ready in: 20 mins.
Serves: 6
Difficulty: easy
Ingredients:
For salad:

- 1 tsp. of Sea salt
- 1 lb. of Ground beef
- 1/4 tsp. of Black pepper
- 1 cup of Tomatoes (chopped)
- 8 oz. of chopped Romaine lettuce (or iceberg lettuce)
- 3/4 cup of shredded Cheddar cheese
- Sesame seeds (optional, to garnish)
- 1/2 cup of Pickles (diced)

For dressing:

- 2 tbsp. of Pickles (diced)
- 1/2 cup of Mayonnaise
- 2 tsp. of Mustard
- 1/2 tsp. of Smoked paprika
- 1 tsp. of White vinegar

- 1 1/2 tbsp. of Besti Monk Powder (or sugar-free or regular honey; as per taste)

Directions:

- In a large pan set over medium-high heat, add the ground meat. (If necessary, you may add a little oil.) Salt and pepper to taste, then shatter with a spatula. Sauté the beef, turning periodically, for 8 to 10 minutes or until it has browned and lost all of its liquid.
- Blend the dressing ingredients together in the meanwhile; if the dressing is too thick, thin it with oil or water before re-puréeing. To taste, adjust the sweetener. Keep chilled until you're ready to serve.
- Combine the tomatoes, lettuce, shredded cheese, & pickles in a big bowl.
- Beef ground up is added. On top of the salad, drizzle the dressing. Coat by tossing.
- If desired, add sesame seeds as a garnish.

Nutritional values per serving:
Total Calories: 368kcal, **Fat:** 31g, **Carbohydrates:** 3g, **Protein:** 18g

3. Broccoli Bacon Salad

Ready in: 10 mins.
Serves: 8
Difficulty: easy
Ingredients:
For broccoli salad:

- 1/4 Red onion, large (finely chopped)
- 1 bunch of Broccoli (chopped in small florets)
- 1/4 cup of cooked Bacon bits
- 1/2 cup of Sunflower seeds
- 1/2 cup of shredded Cheddar cheese
- 1 large cubed Avocado

For dressing:

- 1 tbsp. of Olive oil
- 3/4 cup of Mayonnaise
- 2 tsp. of White vinegar
- 2 tbsp. of Besti Monk Powder (optional, as per taste)
- 1/2 tsp. of Garlic salt
- 1 pinch of Black pepper (optional)

Directions:

- Combine the red onion, broccoli, bacon pieces, sunflower seeds, & cheddar cheese in a large bowl.
- Mayonnaise, white vinegar, olive oil, garlic salt, Besti powder, and pepper should be well combined in a small basin. Mix the dressing in the mixture of vegetables till thoroughly integrated.
- The avocado should be added just before serving.

Nutritional values per serving:
Total Calories: 355kcal, **Fat:** 31g, **Carbohydrates:** 10g, **Protein:** 8g

4. Potato Cauliflower Salad

Ready in: 15 mins.
Serves: 5
Difficulty: easy
Ingredients:

- 2/3 cup of Mayonnaise
- 1 large head of Cauliflower (cut in small florets)
- 1 tbsp. of Apple cider vinegar

- 1/2 tsp. of Garlic powder
- 1 tbsp. of Dijon mustard
- 1/2 tsp. of Paprika
- 1/4 tsp. of Black pepper
- 1/2 tsp. of Sea salt
- 1/3 cup of Onion (finely diced)
- 2 Eggs, large (chopped, hard-boiled)
- 1/3 cup of finely diced Celery
- Chives (to garnish, optional)

Directions:

- Either on the stovetop or in the microwave, cook the cauliflower.
- Salt the water in a saucepan and bring it to a boil. Add the cauliflower, & cook till very tender (about 4-5 minutes). Drain well.

Nutritional values per serving:
Total Calories: 250kcal, **Fat:** 21g, **Carbohydrates:** 11g, **Protein:** 6g

5. Chicken Salad

Ready in: 10 mins.
Serves: 6
Difficulty: easy
Ingredients:

- 2 tbsp. of Mustard
- 1/4 cup of Mayonnaise
- 2 tbsp. of chopped Fresh dill
- 2 cloves of Garlic (minced)
- 2 tbsp. of chopped Fresh parsley
- 3 cups of cooked Shredded chicken
- Sea salt
- 1/2 cup of chopped Green onions
- Black pepper

Directions:

- Mayonnaise, mustard, fresh parsley, fresh dill, and garlic are all combined until smooth.
- Add the chicken & green onions after mixing. To taste, seasoned with black pepper and sea salt.
- To let the flavors meld, place in the refrigerator for at least 2 hours before serving.

Nutritional values per serving:
Total Calories: 175kcal, **Fat:** 12g, **Carbohydrates:** 1g, **Protein:** 16g

6. Chicken Avocado Salad

Ready in: 10 mins.
Serves: 5
Difficulty: easy
Ingredients:

- 2 tbsp. of Lime juice
- 2 Avocados, medium
- Sea salt (as per taste)

- 2 cups of Shredded chicken
- Black pepper (as per taste)
- 1/3 cup of diced Red onion
- 1 tbsp. of minced Jalapenos
- 1/4 cup of chopped Fresh cilantro

Directions:

- Combine the avocado & lime juice in a bowl and season with salt and pepper to taste.
- Red onion, cilantro, jalapenos, and chopped-up chicken should all be added (if using). Combine all of the ingredients. Serve right away.

Nutritional values per serving:
Total Calories: 218kcal, **Fat:** 15g, **Carbohydrates:** 8g, **Protein:** 14g

7. Smoked Salmon Salad

Ready in: 10 mins.
Serves: 4
Difficulty: easy
Ingredients:

- 4 oz. of Smoked salmon (in bite-sized pieces)
- 12 oz. of chopped kale or any other greens you like
- 1 cup of Blueberries
- 1/2 medium cubed Avocado
- 1/3 cup of shelled Pistachios

For dressing:

- 1 tbsp. of Olive oil
- 1/4 cup of Mayonnaise
- 1 tbsp. of Lemon juice
- 2 tbsp. of Honey
- 1/4 tsp. of Garlic powder
- 1 tsp. of Poppy seeds (optional)

Directions:

- In a large salad dish, mix greens smoked salmon, and blueberries.
- All dressing components should be whisked together until emulsified. Mix the salad and dressing together.
- Toss one more time after adding the chopped avocado and pistachios.

Nutritional values per serving:
Total Calories: 317kcal, **Fat:** 25g, **Carbohydrates:** 14g, **Protein:** 10g

8. Stuffed Avocado Salad

Ready in: 15 mins.
Serves: 4
Difficulty: easy
Ingredients:

- 4 slices of Bacon
- 4 Avocado (medium)
- 1 cup of halved Grape tomatoes
- 2 tsp. of Lime juice
- 1 cup of chopped Romaine lettuce
- 1/2 tsp. of Garlic powder
- 1/4 tsp. of Black pepper
- 1/2 tsp. of Sea salt

Directions:

- When the pan is still cold, add the bacon to it. Over medium heat, cook the bacon until crisp, tossing regularly, for approximately 5 to 6 minutes. Dry off with paper towels.
- Cut the avocados in 2 pieces & remove the pits as you wait. Scoop off half of the flesh from each avocado of the half (leave the other half alone), then place in a bowl.
- The avocado should be mixed with garlic powder, lime juice, and sea

salt. Using a fork, mash. If necessary, taste and adjust the spices.

- Add lettuce and cherry tomatoes after folding.
- Chop up the bacon pieces and put them in the basin after they are cold enough to handle.
- Refill the avocado halves with the mixture by scooping. Add freshly cracked pepper to the top, if preferred.

Nutritional values per serving:
Total Calories: 189kcal, **Fat:** 16g, **Carbohydrates:** 10g, **Protein:** 4g

9. Spicy Kani Salad

Ready in: 10 mins.
Serves: 4
Difficulty: easy
Ingredients:
For salad:

- 12 oz. of Kelp noodles (rinsed in hot water till soft)
- 8 oz. of Lump crab meat
- 1/2 cup of Carrots (cut in matchstick pieces)
- 1/2 cup of Cucumber (cut into matchstick pieces)

For dressing:

- 1 tsp. of Lemon juice
- 1/4 cup of Mayonnaise
- 1 tsp. of Sriracha (to taste)
- 1 tsp. of Toasted sesame oil

Directions:

- All dressing components should be whipped together. (Do this in advance & put it in the refrigerator until just before serving for optimal flavor development.)
- Combine the crab meat, kelp noodles, cucumber, and carrots. Add the dressing and stir. Add salt & black pepper to taste if necessary.
- Use fish roe or sesame seeds as a garnish (optional).

Nutritional values per serving:
Total Calories: 169kcal, **Fat:** 12g, **Carbohydrates:** 4g, **Protein:** 12g

10. Buffalo Chicken Salad

Ready in: 10 mins.
Serves: 5
Difficulty: easy
Ingredients:

- 1/2 cup of Ranch dressing
- 4 cups of Shredded chicken
- 2 oz. of crumbled Blue cheese
- 1/2 cup of diced Celery
- 1/3 cup of Buffalo sauce
- 1/3 cup of sliced Green onions

Directions:

- Add the ranch dressing, shredded chicken, blue cheese, celery dice, buffalo sauce, and green onions to a large bowl. Mix the ingredients well by stirring.
- Once you're ready to eat, chill into the refrigerator to allow the flavors to meld.

Nutritional values per serving:
Total Calories: 355kcal, **Fat:** 24g, **Carbohydrates:** 1g, **Protein:** 30g

CHAPTER 7:
Keto Diet - Desserts and Drinks Recipes
Desserts

1. Cream Cheese Cookies

Ready in: 25 mins.
Serves: 24
Difficulty: easy
Ingredients:

- 2 oz. of softened Cream cheese
- 1/4 cup of butter, unsalted (softened)
- 1/3 cup of Besti Monk Blend
- 1 tsp. of Vanilla extract
- 1 Egg, large (at room temperature)
- 1/4 tsp. of Sea salt
- 3 cups of Almond Flour
- 1 tbsp. of Sour cream (optional)

Directions:

- Set the oven up to 350 degrees Fahrenheit (177 degrees C). Using parchment paper, line a big cookie sheet.
- The cream cheese, butter, and sweetener should be combined with a stand mixer or hand mixer until frothy & light in color.
- Add salt, egg, and vanilla essence after beating. If using, beat sour cream in (optional).
- At a time, add 1/2 cup (64 g) of the almond flour by beating. It will be a soft dough. Refrigerate for 25-30 minutes if, when touched, it adheres to your hands.
- Scoop dough balls onto the prepped cookie sheet using a standard cookie scoop (approximately 1 1/2 tablespoons, 22 mL volume). Flatten using your palm.
- Bake for 12 to 15 minutes or until the sides are just beginning to turn brown. Before handling, let the pan cool fully.

Nutritional values per serving:
Total Calories: 110kcal, **Fat:** 10g, **Carbohydrates:** 3g, **Protein:** 3g

2. Almond Flour Blueberry Muffins

Ready in: 30 mins.
Serves: 12
Difficulty: easy
Ingredients:

- 1/2 cup of Besti Monk Blend
- 2 1/2 cups of Almond Flour
- 1 1/2 tsp. of Baking powder
- 1/3 cup of Coconut oil (melted)
- 1/4 tsp. of Sea salt (optional)

- 1/3 cup of almond milk, unsweetened (at room temperature)
- 1/2 tsp. of Vanilla extract
- 3 Eggs, large (at room temperature)
- 3/4 cup of Blueberries

Directions:

- Set the oven up to 350 degrees Fahrenheit (177 degrees C). 10 to 12 parchment paper or silicone muffin liners should be used to line a muffin tray. (Use 12 if you want fewer calories and carbohydrates, or 10 if you want bigger muffin tops.)
- Mix the Besti, almond flour, baking soda, and sea salt in a large basin.
- Melted coconut oil, eggs, almond milk, and vanilla essence should all be combined. Add the blueberries and stir.
- Fill each muffin cup with an equal amount of the batter. The top should be brown, and a toothpick inserted should come out clean after 20 to 25 minutes of baking.

Nutritional values per serving:
Total Calories: 217kcal, **Fat:** 19g, **Carbohydrates:** 6g, **Protein:** 7g

3. Cheesecake

Ready in: 1 hr. 10 mins.
Serves: 16
Difficulty: easy
Ingredients:
For crust:

- 1/3 cup of butter, unsalted (then melted)
- 2 cups of Almond Flour
- 1 tsp. of Vanilla extract
- 2 tbsp. of Besti Monk Blend (powdered or granular works fine)

For filling:

- 1 1/4 cups of Besti Monk Powder
- 32 oz. of softened Cream cheese
- 3 Eggs (large)
- 1 tsp. of Vanilla extract
- 1 tbsp. of Lemon juice

Directions:

- Set the oven up to 350 degrees Fahrenheit (177 degrees C). Using parchment paper, line a 9-inch springform pan.
- Almond flour, Besti, melted butter, and vanilla essence is blended in a medium bowl to create the cheesecake crust. The dough would be a little bit brittle.
- The prepared pan's bottom should be pressed with the dough. Bake for 10 to 12 minutes or until just beginning to turn brown. Let it at least 10 mins to cool.

Filling:

- Cream cheese & powdered sugar should be frothy after being combined at low speed.
- One at a time beat in the eggs.
- Lemon juice & vanilla essence should be beaten in. (Continue mixing at a low to medium speed; too high a speed would result in excess of air bubbles, which is not what we want.)

Assembly:

- Over the crust, pour the filling into the pan. Make the top smooth using a spatula. Tap the pan onto the counter several times to make sure there are no air bubbles.

- When the middle is nearly set but still jiggly, bake for approximately 40 to 55 minutes.
- Cheesecake should be taken out of the oven. Run a knife over the edge of the sides stuck into the pan, but leave the springform edge on. After fully set, chill for at least 4 hours (ideally overnight) in the refrigerator after cooling in the pan onto the counter to room temperature. Prior to chilling, do not attempt to take the cake out of the pan.

Nutritional values per serving:
Total Calories: 325kcal, **Fat:** 31g, **Carbohydrates:** 6g, **Protein:** 7g

4. Almond Milk Ice Cream

Ready in: 4 hr. 35 mins.
Serves: 6
Difficulty: easy
Ingredients:

- 3 cups of Heavy cream (split into 2 cups & 1 cup)
- 3 tbsp. of unsalted butter
- 1/3 cup of Besti Monk Powder
- 1 cup of almond milk, unsweetened
- 2 tsp. of Vanilla extract

Directions:

- Over medium heat, melt the butter into a large skillet or sauté pan (not a saucepan!).
- 2 cups heavy cream and Besti powder should be added. Bring to a boil before simmering. Stirring periodically, simmer for 30-45 minutes or until the liquid is thick (as condensed milk), coats the backside of a spoon, and has decreased in volume by half. When you tilt it, it will also start to peel away from the pan. (Using a bigger pan can speed up the process.)
- Condensed milk should be poured into a big dish and let to chill until room temperature. Add the vanilla essence and stir.
- Blend the remaining heavy cream and almond milk together.
- The mixture should be refrigerated for at least 4-5 hours or overnight. (If you absolutely want to, you may skip this step, however, chilling it will improve the texture.)

Nutritional values per serving:
Total Calories: 467kcal, **Fat:** 49g, **Carbohydrates:** 3g, **Protein:** 3g

5. Fudgy Brownies

Ready in: 25 mins.
Serves: 16
Difficulty: easy

Ingredients:

- 4 oz. of baking chocolate, unsweetened
- 1/2 cup of unsalted butter
- 3/4 cup of Almond Flour
- 2 tbsp. of Cocoa powder
- 2/3 cup of Besti Powder
- 2 Eggs, large (at room temperature)
- 1/4 tsp. of Sea salt
- 1 tsp. of Vanilla extract (optional)
- 1/4 cup of chopped Walnuts (optional)

Directions:

- Set the oven up to 350 degrees Fahrenheit (177 degrees C). Using parchment paper, line a pan (8x8 in), extending the paper's edges over the sides.
- In a double boiler, combine the butter & chocolate and melt them together until smooth. Get rid of the heat.
- Add the vanilla essence and stir.
- Add the eggs, sea salt, cocoa powder, and almond flour in powder form. Combine and combine until uniform. The batter will seem somewhat gritty.
- Put the batter in the prepared pan. Use the backside of a spoon or a spatula to level the top. Add chopped walnuts & press them into the top, if preferred.
- Bake for roughly 13 to 18 minutes, or until a toothpick inserted into the center of the cake comes out spotless but with a small amount of batter still clinging to it. (Don't wait to get completely clean, & don't worry if any butter pools on top; focus instead on making sure the brownie portion is extremely soft but not liquid.)
- Cool thoroughly before attempting to move or cut. Butter may have accumulated on top; do not drain it; it will blend back in once the food has cooled.

Nutritional values per serving:
Total Calories: 174kcal, **Fat:** 16g, **Carbohydrates:** 4g, **Protein:** 3g

6. Peanut Butter Cookies

Ready in: 25 mins.
Serves: 27
Difficulty: easy
Ingredients:

- 2 Eggs, large
- 1 1/4 cups of Peanut butter (salted, creamy & not too runny)
- 1/3 cup of Besti Monk Blend

Optional:

- 1/4 tsp. of Sea salt
- 1 tsp. of Vanilla extract
- 3/4 cup of Peanuts (coarsely chopped)

Directions:

- Set the oven up to 350 degrees Fahrenheit (177 degrees C). Use parchment paper to cover a baking sheet.
- In a food processor, combine the Besti, peanut butter, vanilla extract (if used), and salt (if used). Process until uniform, stopping to scrape the sides as necessary.
- If used, pulse into the peanut pieces just long enough to mix them. (Avoid over-mixing; some bits should remain for crunch.)
- To distribute dough balls on the prepped cookie sheet, use a cookie scoop. Before releasing it onto the sheet, firmly press your cookie dough in the scoop. Use a criss-crossing motion with a fork to flatten. The fork should be cleaned using a paper towel in between cookies after being dipped in a cup of cold water. (Doing so will stop sticking.)
- Bake for 15 to 20 minutes or until just barely brown. Totally cool before handling. When they cool, cookies will become crisp.

Nutritional values per serving:
Total Calories: 102kcal, **Fat:** 8g, **Carbohydrates:** 2g, **Protein:** 4g

7. Pound Cake

Ready in: 1 hr. 15 mins.
Serves: 16
Difficulty: easy
Ingredients:

- 1 cup of Besti Erythritol
- 3/4 cup of butter, unsalted (softened)
- 4 Eggs, large (at room temperature)
- 2 tbsp. of Lemon extract
- 3/4 cup of Sour cream
- 2 tsp. of Vanilla extract (optional)
- 2 tsp. of Baking powder
- 3 cups of Almond Flour
- 1/2 tsp. of Sea salt
- 3 tbsp. Of Poppy seeds

For the lemon glaze:

- 1/4 cup of Lemon juice
- 3/4 cup of Besti Powder
- 1/4 tsp. of Vanilla extract (optional)

Directions:

- Set the oven up to 350 degrees Fahrenheit (177 degrees C). Bundt pan prepared; put aside.
- Use a hand mixer to whip the butter & sweetener to a frothy consistency in a large bowl.
- Add the eggs, lemon, sour cream and vanilla extracts, and beat well.
- Combine the baking soda, almond flour, poppy seeds, & sea salt in a separate bowl. One cup at a time beat the dry components into the wet components.
- Smooth the top of the batter after transferring it to the pan. The top should be a deep golden brown after approximately 40 minutes of baking. Loosely cover with foil and bake for a further 20 to 35 minutes, till a toothpick inserted into the center comes out clean. Let it cool in the pan for 15 minutes at least, then

remove it and allow cool fully on a cooling rack.

- Lemon juice, vanilla essence, and powdered sugar should be whipped together to produce the glaze. Pour a drizzle on the cake.

Nutritional values per serving:
Total Calories: 248kcal, **Fat:** 23g, **Carbohydrates:** 6g, **Protein:** 7g

8. Red Velvet Cake

Ready in: 45 mins.
Serves: 24
Difficulty: easy
Ingredients:

- 1 1/2 cups of Besti Monk Blend
- 3/4 cup of softened Salted butter
- 3 Eggs, large (at normal temperature)
- 3/4 cup of Sour cream (at normal temperature)
- 1 tbsp. of Vanilla extract
- 1/2 cup of almond milk, unsweetened (at normal temperature)
- 3 cups of Almond Flour
- 1 tsp. of White vinegar
- 2 tbsp. of Cocoa powder
- 2 tbsp. of Beetroot powder
- 2 tsp. of Baking soda

For frosting:

- Pecans, chopped (optional; to top)
- 3 1/2 cups of Cream Cheese Frosting

Directions:

- Set the oven up to 350 degrees Fahrenheit (177 degrees C). Put parchment paper in the bottom of two 9" round springform pans.
- Beat Besti and butter together until frothy in a large bowl.
- One at a time beat in the eggs. To avoid splashing, stir the sour cream, vanilla, almond milk, & vinegar in first, then beat to combine.
- Beat the almond flour in, 1/2 cup at a time, with the mixer set on low. When the mixture is smooth, add baking soda and cocoa powder. To get the appropriate hue, beat beetroot powder in, if using, one tsp at a time.
- Distribute the dough across the two pans, then use a spatula to level the surface. Bake for about 20-25 minutes, or until a toothpick inserted comes out clean. Cool entirely in the pans, & flip to release by running a knife down the edges.
- To make the cream cheese frosting, use the directions found here.
- Put 1 coat of cake on a dish or cake stand. Use 3/4 cup of frosting to decorate the top. Put the top layer on top & cover with an additional 3/4 cup of icing (255 g). Lastly,

spread 1 1/2 cups of icing around the edges. Top with some chopped pecans if desired.

Nutritional values per serving:
Total Calories: 286kcal, **Fat:** 27g, **Carbohydrates:** 5g, **Protein:** 5g

9. Pecan Pie

Ready in: 1 hr. 20 mins.
Serves: 12
Difficulty: easy
Ingredients:

- 3/4 cup of unsalted butter
- 1 pie crust, Almond flour
- 3/4 cup of Besti Powder
- 1 tsp. of Sea salt
- 1 1/2 cups of Heavy cream
- 1/2 tbsp. of Vanilla extract
- 1 Egg, large (at room temperature)
- 3/4 tsp. of Maple extract
- 2 1/2 cups of Pecans (2 cups coarsely chopped plus 1/2 cup of halves for topping)

Directions:

- Set the oven up to 350 degrees Fahrenheit (177 degrees C).
- Follow the directions on this page to make the pie crust using almond flour.
- Make the filler in the interim. Heat the butter & Besti for approximately 5 minutes, stirring often, till dark golden brown in a big sauté pan.
- Add the cream & sea salt until golden. Bring to a simmering boil. Simmer until bubbling, dark golden, and thick, about 15 to 20 minutes. A spoon should be covered with caramel sauce.
- Take the sauce off the heat. Add the vanilla & maple extracts and stir.
- Let the pie crust & caramel sauce warm up for 15-20 minutes, but not to a boiling point. You may either keep the oven on while they cool (you'll need it again) or, when the cooling period is nearly up, rewarm it to 350 ° F (177 degrees C).
- Add the egg after the caramel sauce gets cooled sufficiently (warm is OK) so that it won't fry it.
- Sprinkle the crust equally with the chopped pecans. Over the pecans, pour the caramel/egg mixture. Add half of pecan on top.
- Foil the pie crust edges, leaving the middle unblocked.
- Bake for about 30 to 35 minutes or until the filling is bubbling, thick, and nearly set on top.
- To set, let cool fully. Before slicing, freeze for at least an hour for optimal results.

Nutritional values per serving:
Total Calories: 533kcal, **Fat:** 54g, **Carbohydrates:** 8g, **Protein:** 9g

10. Apple Pie

Ready in: 1 hr. 35 mins.
Serves: 12
Difficulty: easy
Ingredients:
For Pie filling:

- 1/4 cup of Besti Powder
- 1/2 cup of butter, unsalted
- 6 tbsp. of Lemon juice (divided)
- 1 tsp. of Nutmeg
- 2 tsp. of Cinnamon

- 1/2 tsp. of Cardamom
- 5 Yellow squash, medium (peeled, sliced & diced into half-inch pieces)
- 1 tbsp. of gelatin powder, unflavored
- 1/2 tsp. of Maple extract (optional)
- 1 tsp. of Vanilla extract (optional)

For pie crust:

- 3 3/4 cups of Almond Flour
- 1/3 cup of Besti Monk Blend
- 1/2 tsp. of Sea salt
- 1/2 cup of butter, unsalted (measured solid & melted)
- 1 Egg, large
- 1/2 tsp. of Vanilla extract (optional)
- 1 tbsp. of gelatin powder, unflavored
- 2 tbsp. of Water

Directions:

- 3 tbsp. (44 mL) of lemon juice should be mixed with the gelatin powder in a little pinch bowl. Let alone grow.
- Melt the butter in a big 3.5-quart (3.3 liters) pot over medium heat. Add the remaining 3 tbsp. (44 mL) of lemon juice, powdered sweetener, cinnamon, nutmeg, & cardamom. Whisk the gelatin mixture into the pan after it has thickened until it has completely dissolved.
- To the pan, add the cubed squash. Simmer for a while. Simmer the mixture for 30 to 40 minutes over medium heat or until it has thickened to the consistency of apple pie filling and the squash is extremely tender.
- Add the vanilla & maple extracts and stir.
- Let the filling cool for at least 20 minutes or until it is no hotter than lukewarm.

Apple pie:

- In the meanwhile, heat oven to 350°F (177 degrees C).
- Follow steps 1 through 3 from this recipe for an almond flour pie crust, but substitute the quantities of butter, egg, vanilla, sweetener, and almond flour listed above. (This additional sum is for the topmost crust.)
- With a hand mixer, blend the water and gelatin powder until evenly distributed.
- Dough is divided in half. In the pie pan that has been prepared, press half of the dough into the bottom and up the sides. Separate the second half of the dough.
- The crust should only be gently browned after 10 to 12 minutes in the oven.
- After completing, let it cool for ten minutes at least before incorporating the filling.
- In the meanwhile, sandwich the other half of dough between two sheets of parchment paper that have been gently greased. Roll out the top crust to a circle that is just a bit bigger than the topmost of the pie pan using parchment paper as a surface.

Apple pie assembly:

- If the oven has cooled, re-heat it to 350°F (177 degrees C). When assembling, make sure the filling &

bottom crust are both no hotter than lukewarm.

- Transfer the chilled filling carefully over the chilled bottom crust.
- Remove the top parchment paper layer from the top crust that has been rolled out. Flip the top-most crust onto the pie using the piece of parchment paper at the bottom, then quickly and gently peel the parchment paper off. Make sure the top crust still fully encloses the bottom crust before trimming any extra off the sides using a knife. To seal the edges, push them down with your fingertips. Make 4 cuts at the top of the pie.
- Till the edges are browned, bake for 20 to 25 minutes. When the top-most crust is lightly brown and feels semi-firm to the touch, cover the pie's edges with foil & bake for another 5 to 15 minutes. (It won't completely firm up until it has cooled.)
- Before removing or cutting from the pan, take the pie out of the oven and allow it to cool fully.

Nutritional values per serving:
Total Calories: 363kcal, **Fat:** 33g, **Carbohydrates:** 12g, **Protein:** 10g

11. Banana Pudding

Ready in: 40 mins.
Serves: 12
Difficulty: easy
Ingredients:

- 1 cup of Whipped Cream

Banana pudding layer:

- 1/2 cup of Besti Powder
- 2 cups of Heavy cream
- 1/4 tsp. of Sea salt
- 1/2 tsp. of Xanthan gum
- 5 Egg yolks, large
- 2 tsp. of Banana extract
- 1/4 cup of butter, unsalted (at room temperature)
- 1 tsp. of Vanilla extract

Shortbread cookie:

- Shortbread Cookies dough, Coconut Flour

Directions:

- In a saucepan on medium heat, combine the heavy cream, Besti, and sea salt for the banana pudding. Simmer for a while.
- In the meanwhile, mix the egg yolks in a medium bowl.
- While the cream is heating, whisk continuously as you gently pour 1/2 cup of the mixture of hot cream into the egg yolks. Tempering is the term for this.
- Return the warm egg yolk mixture to the pan. Sprinkle the xanthan gum evenly (don't throw it on top), then whisk quickly to mix. Cook the mixture for 4-5 minutes or until it thickens.
- Remove from heat & whisk the vanilla extract, banana essence, and butter.
- Ten minutes should be allowed for the pudding to cool. Push the plastic wrap onto the top of the mixture of pudding to avoid a film from developing. Whisk the mixture one

more to remove the film on top before covering it. Refrigerate until hard, at least two hours.

A layer of shortbread cookies:

- Make your shortbread cookies as directed here while the pudding rests in the refrigerator.

Assembly:

- Coconut flour shortbread biscuits in one layer should be used to line a 9 x 13-inch baking dish.

Follow these directions to make the whipped cream:

- Use a spatula to delicately incorporate one cup of the whipping cream in the pudding mixture.
- Overlay the cookies into the baking dish with the pudding mixture.
- Over the pudding layer, dot the remaining whipped cream.
- If wanted, you may garnish with any leftover shortbread cookies and banana slices.
- To thoroughly set, cover and chill for 4 hours at least or ideally overnight.

Nutritional values per serving:
Total Calories: 443kcal, **Fat:** 44g, **Carbohydrates:** 8g, **Protein:** 5g

12. Peanut Butter Mousse

Ready in: 10 mins.
Serves: 4
Difficulty: easy
Ingredients:

- 1/4 cup of Peanut butter
- 3/4 cup of Heavy cream
- 3 tbsp. of Besti Powder
- Chocolate sauce, Sugar-free (optional)
- 1/2 cup of Mascarpone cheese (at normal temperature)

Directions:

- Use a hand mixer to whip the heavy cream in a large bowl for 3 to 4 minutes or until soft peaks form. To use later, take off 1/4 of whipped cream & save it.
- Mascarpone cheese and peanut butter should be blended to a creamy consistency in a small bowl. Add the Besti powder and stir until fully combined.
- Gently incorporate the whipped cream into the mixture of peanut butter while being mindful not to overwork the whipped cream.
- Scoop the mousse into serving bowls, then top with a dab of the leftover whipped cream, chocolate sauce, or both.

Nutritional values per serving:
Total Calories: 380kcal, **Fat:** 36g, **Carbohydrates:** 4g, **Protein:** 7g

13. Donuts

Ready in: 30 mins.
Serves: 6
Difficulty: easy
Ingredients:

- 1/4 cup of Besti Monk Blend
- 1 cup of Almond Flour
- 2 tsp. of Baking powder
- 1/8 tsp. of Sea salt
- 1 tsp. of Cinnamon
- 1/4 cup of butter, unsalted (melted plus some more for the pan)

- 2 Eggs, large (at normal temperature)
- 1/4 cup of almond milk, unsweetened (at normal temperature)
- 1/2 cup of Besti Powder (for coating)
- 1/2 tsp. of Vanilla extract

Directions:

- Set the oven to up 350 degrees Fahrenheit (177 degrees C). Ideally, grease a nonstick doughnut pan.
- Combine the Besti, almond flour, baking soda, cinnamon, & sea salt in a big bowl.
- Melted butter, egg, almond milk, and vanilla essence are combined in a small dish. With a whisk, combine the wet and dry ingredients.
- Fill the doughnut cavities with the batter equally, about 3/4 of the way full. Around 15 minutes should be enough time to bake anything till golden brown.
- The pan should be totally cool. The sides of the donuts should be run along with a little silicone spatula, then gently twisted.
- Put Besti Powdered in a little dish with a shallow bottom. Donuts are coated by pressing them into the powder on both sides. (If you'd like, you may substitute a different icing or glaze.

Nutritional values per serving:
Total Calories: 203kcal, **Fat:** 18g, **Carbohydrates:** 5g, **Protein:** 6g

14. Pumpkin Pie

Ready in: 45 mins.
Serves: 8
Difficulty: easy
Ingredients:

- 1/2 cup of Heavy cream
- 1 can of Pumpkin puree (15 oz.)
- 3 Eggs, large (at normal temperature)
- 1/4 cup of Besti Brown Monk Blend
- 1/2 cup of Besti Powder Blend
- 1 tbsp. of Pumpkin pie spice
- 1/2 tbsp. of Vanilla extract (optional)
- 1/4 tsp. of Sea salt
- 2 tsp. of gelatin powder, unflavored

Directions:

- Set the oven up to 300 degrees Fahrenheit (163 degrees C). Use butter or neutral cooking spray to grease a pie tin.
- Beat the pumpkin, eggs, cream, Besti Powder, Besti Brown, sea salt, pumpkin pie spice, and vanilla (if used) in a large bowl with a hand mixer on medium-low speed until creamy. (Avoid over-mixing.)
- Sprinkle the gelatin powder on the batter and start beating right away to achieve uniformity. (If using arrowroot or coconut flour, beat them in the same manner.) Give the batter five minutes to rest.
- Fill the pie tin with the batter. To get any air bubbles out, lightly tap on the counter.
- When you jiggle the pan, the pumpkin pie should still be somewhat jiggly in the middle after 35 to 45 minutes of baking (like jello). With a meat thermometer, the internal

temperature must be between 165 and 170 degrees F. (74-77 degrees C).

- Before slicing, allow the cake to cool fully on the counter, without cover, and then chill in the refrigerator for at least 2 hours (or until very cold).

Nutritional values per serving:
Total Calories: 104kcal, **Fat:** 7g, **Carbohydrates:** 4g, **Protein:** 5g

15. Peach Cobbler

Ready in: 45 mins.
Serves: 9
Difficulty: easy
Ingredients:
For filling:

- 6 tbsp. of Besti Monk Blend
- 5 Peaches, medium (cored, peeled, & sliced)
- 1/8 tsp. of Sea salt
- 1/4 tsp. of Cinnamon (optional)
- 1/4 tsp. of Xanthan gum

For topping:

- 1/4 cup of Besti Monk Blend
- 1 cup of Almond Flour
- 1 tsp. of Baking powder
- 1/4 cup of butter, unsalted (cold)
- 1/4 tsp. of Sea salt
- 1 Egg, large
- 1 tsp. of Vanilla extract
- 2 tbsp. of Heavy cream

Directions:

- Set the oven to 375 degrees F. (176 degrees C).
- The Besti (both normal & brown), peaches, cinnamon, & sea salt should all be combined in a large pot. The peaches should be cooked for approximately 15 minutes over medium heat, stirring regularly, until they soften and release some juice. Based on how sweet the peaches are, taste them and adjust the sweetener as necessary.
- Sprinkle the xanthan gum on the peaches sparingly (do not pour it on top), then stir until the mixture is thickened.
- In a 9 x 9 baking dish, spread the peach filling out in a single layer.
- In a food processor, combine the Besti, almond flour, baking soda, and sea salt until uniform, process.
- Butter should be added. Just pulse sporadically until it crumbles.
- Add the cream, vanilla, and egg. When you mix, pulse.
- With a few exposed areas, drop teaspoons of batter on the peaches into the baking dish, covering the majority of the top.

- Bake for approximately 15 minutes or until golden brown on top.

Nutritional values per serving:
Total Calories: 172kcal, **Fat:** 13g, **Carbohydrates:** 11g, **Protein:** 4g

16. White Chocolate Mousse

Ready in: 10 mins.
Serves: 3
Difficulty: easy
Ingredients:

- ½ cup of White Chocolate Chips
- 1 cup of divided heavy whipping cream

Directions:

- Heat 1/3 cup of heavy whipping cream and white chocolate chips in a microwave-safe dish until the baking chips melt. Depending on the microwave's wattage, this should take 35 to 50 seconds.
- After the white chocolate has fully melted in, stir the warm cream mixture. Set aside.
- Large mixing bowl with remaining 2/3 cup cream added. Beat until firm peaks form.
- Whipping cream should be gradually incorporated into the mixture of white chocolate.
- Refrigerate mousse for at least two hours to allow it to solidify before dividing it among 3 dessert plates.

Nutritional values per serving:
Total Calories: 431kcal, **Fat:** 38g, **Carbohydrates:** 12g, **Protein:** 4g

17. Coconut Custard

Ready in: 1 hr.
Serves: 5
Difficulty: easy
Ingredients:

- ⅓ cup of sugar substitute (low carb) or ½ tsp. of liquid stevia
- 3 eggs
- A dash of salt
- ½ tsp. of vanilla extract
- 2 ¼ cups of coconut milk
- A dash of nutmeg, ground (optional)
- 2 tbsp. of shredded coconut, unsweetened

Directions:

- Salt, sweetener, and eggs should all be whisked together until barely combined.
- Just bring coconut milk to a simmer.
- Whisk warm coconut milk into the egg mixture gradually.
- Add coconut and vanilla essence and stir.
- Into five custard cups, pour. If desired, nutmeg should be added.
- In a 13 by 9 baking pan, put cups. Heat up some water in the pan to approximately 1 inch.
- Do 45 to 50 minutes of baking at 350 degrees F, or till a knife inserted close to the middle comes out clean.
- Remove cups and let them cool on a wire rack for an hour. Put a cover on it and put it in the fridge.

Nutritional values per serving:
Total Calories: 85kcal, **Fat:** 4g, **Carbohydrates:** 2g, **Protein:** 7g

18. Tiramisu Whoopie Pies

Ready in: 35 mins.
Serves: 12
Difficulty: easy
Ingredients:
For Cookies:

- 3 tbsp. of whey protein, unflavored
- 2 cups of almond flour
- ½ cup of Sweetener
- ½ tsp. of baking soda
- 2 tsp. of baking powder
- ½ tsp. of salt
- ½ cup of sugar substitute (low carb)
- ½ cup of butter in small cubes
- 2 eggs (large)
- ½ cup of sour cream, full fat
- 1 tsp. of vanilla extract
- cocoa powder, to dust

For Filling:

- 1 tbsp. of dark rum
- ¼ cup of cold espresso coffee
- 8 ounces of mascarpone cheese
- A pinch salt
- 2 tbsp. of sugar substitute, low carb
- ½ cup of heavy cream
- 2 tsp. of dark rum (optional)
- 2 tsp. of vanilla extract

Directions:

- Set the oven up to 350 °F. Apply non-stick spray to the whoopie pie pan.
- In a bowl, combine the following ingredients: salt, baking soda, baking powder, protein powder, and brown sugar sweetener. Set aside.
- With a mixer, beat the butter and sugar for two minutes on medium-high speed till creamy. Beat in the eggs & 1 teaspoon of vanilla after adding them. Clean the bowl's sides with a scraper. Add the sour cream before the dry mixture.
- Fill each whoopie pie form with approximately two-thirds of the batter using a tiny teaspoon. Sprinkle a little chocolate powder above each batter scoop after placing some in a tiny sieve.
- Bake for 10 to 12 minutes or until sides are brown.
- After approximately 10 minutes of cooling on a wire rack, take the cookies from the pan and let them cool. (Cookies that aren't filled may be kept for up to a day.)
- Turn the cookies upside-down on a rack after they have cooled.
- In a small dish, combine 3 tablespoons of dark rum and espresso. Each cookie's bottom side should have around 1/4 tsp. of espresso liquid spread on it.
- Mascarpone cheese, low-carb sugar alternative, salt, heavy cream, vanilla, and 1 teaspoon of black rum should be blended together with a mixer. Pour part of the mascarpone cheese mixture over the cookies' chocolate half. Add the second cookie half to the top. Serve right away or store in the refrigerator. (These cookies may also be stored in the freezer after being individually wrapped in plastic.)

Nutritional values per serving:
Total Calories: 344kcal, **Fat:** 32g, **Carbohydrates:** 8g, **Protein:** 10g

19. Apple Crisp

Ready in: 1 hr. 5 mins.
Serves: 9
Difficulty: easy
Ingredients:
For filling:

- 3 tbsp. of lemon juice
- 6 cups of peeled zucchini, sliced
- ⅔ cup of sugar substitute (low carb)
- ½ tsp. of ground nutmeg
- ¾ tsp. of ground cinnamon
- 1 tsp. of apple extract (optional)
- ¼ tsp. of xanthan gum (optional thickener)

For topping:

- ½ cup of almond flour
- ½ cup of chopped pecans
- ¼ cup of oat fiber or coconut flour
- 1 tsp. of cinnamon
- ¼ cup of sugar substitute (low carb)
- ¼ cup of butter

Directions:

- Zucchini, sweetener, lemon juice, cinnamon, and nutmeg should all be well mixed in a medium basin. Add apple extract as well for a richer apple flavor. Fill a prepared 9 x 9-inch baking dish with the ingredients.
- Mix nuts, oat fiber, almond flour, sugar, & cinnamon into a bowl to make the topping, and then chop in butter until it forms a crumbly texture. Sprinkle on top of the mixture of zucchini.
- Bake zucchini for 45–50 minutes at 350°F or until soft.

Nutritional values per serving:
Total Calories: 149kcal, **Fat:** 13g, **Carbohydrates:** 7g, **Protein:** 3g

20. Coconut Lemon Cream Cheese Balls

Ready in: 5 mins.
Serves: 12
Difficulty: easy
Ingredients:

- 4 ounces of softened cream cheese
- ½ cup of blanched almond flour
- 2 tbsp. of Monk Fruit blend
- 3 tbsp. of shredded coconut, unsweetened
- 2-3 tbsp. of fresh lemon juice

Directions:

- In a food processor, combine the cream cheese, almond flour, monk fruit sweetener, & lemon juice.
- Mix till it becomes a homogeneous dough, then shape into 12-13 balls by hand.
- Place the balls onto a baking sheet after rolling them in the coconut.
- Store in the fridge in an airtight container after chilling until solid.

Nutritional values per serving:
Total Calories: 71kcal, **Fat:** 6g, **Carbohydrates:** 1g, **Protein:** 1g

Drinks

1. Chocolate Milk

Ready in: 5 mins.
Serves: 4
Difficulty: easy
Ingredients:

- 2/3 cup of Heavy cream
- 3 1/3 cups of almond milk, Unsweetened
- 6 tbsp. of Cocoa powder
- 2 tsp. of Vanilla extract
- 6 tbsp. of Besti Powder

Directions:

- All components should be blended in a blender until smooth.

Nutritional values per serving:
Total Calories: 179kcal, **Fat:** 17g, **Carbohydrates:** 6g, **Protein:** 3g

2. Pina Colada

Ready in: 5 mins.
Serves: 2
Difficulty: easy
Ingredients:

- 1/2 cup of Coconut cream
- 3 oz. of Rum
- 1/2 cup of Pineapple chunks
- 1/4 cup of Besti Powder Monk Blend
- 1/2 tsp. of Pineapple extract (optional)
- 3 cups of Ice

Directions:

- Blend together Besti, rum, pineapple pieces, coconut cream, pineapple essence, and ice in a blender.
- All components should be well combined.

Nutritional values per serving:
Total Calories: 332kcal, **Fat:** 21g, **Carbohydrates:** 13g, **Protein:** 3g

3. Slush

Ready in: 5 mins.
Serves: 3
Difficulty: easy
Ingredients:

- 1 1/4 cups of Sparkling water

- 2 1/2 cups of mixed berries, Frozen (strawberries, blueberries, raspberries, and/or blackberries)
- 1/4 cup of Besti Powder Blend

Directions:

- In a blender, combine all the ingredients.
- Once smooth, blend.

Nutritional values per serving:
Total Calories: 54kcal, **Fat:** 0g, **Carbohydrates:** 12g, **Protein:** 1g

4. Skinny Margarita

Ready in: 5 mins.
Serves: 4
Difficulty: easy
Ingredients:

- 1/3 cup of Lime juice (freshly squeezed)
- 6 fl. Oz. of Tequila
- 1 1/2 tsp. of Orange extract
- 5 cups of Ice cubes
- 3 tbsp. of Besti Powder Blend
- Lime wedges (to garnish)
- Sea salt

Directions:

- In a strong blender, combine all the ingredients (apart from lime wedges and sea salt). Use the ice crush option to blend until a slushy consistency is achieved. If necessary, add more ice to create a total of 32 fl. oz.
- Each glass's rim should be covered with a lime slice. Dip your rim into a small bowl or plate that is salted. Fill the cups with frozen margaritas and top with lime slices.

Nutritional values per serving:
Total Calories: 106kcal, **Fat:** 0g, **Carbohydrates:** 1g, **Protein:** 0g

5. Matcha Green Frappe

Ready in: 5 mins.
Serves: 1
Difficulty: easy
Ingredients:

- 2 tbsp. of Heavy cream
- 3/4 cup of almond milk, unsweetened
- 1/2 tbsp. of Matcha Green Tea
- 1 tbsp. of Besti Powder (optional)
- 1 cup of Ice
- Whipped cream, Sugar-free (optional), to top
- 1/2 tsp. of Vanilla extract (optional)

Directions:

- Blend everything in a blender except the whipped cream. Mix until you have the consistency you want.
- If desired, taste and adjust sweetener or matcha.
- Into a jar or glass, pour. Add whipped cream over the top.

Nutritional values per serving:
Total Calories: 156kcal, **Fat:** 13g, **Carbohydrates:** 2g, **Protein:** 5g

6. Peanut Butter Chocolate Smoothie

Ready in: 5 mins.
Serves: 3
Difficulty: easy
Ingredients:

- 3 tbsp. of Cocoa powder
- 1/4 cup of creamy Peanut butter
- 1 cup of Heavy cream
- 6 tbsp. of Besti Powder Erythritol (as per taste)
- 1 1/2 cups of almond milk, unsweetened (vanilla or regular)
- 1/8 tsp. of Sea salt (optional)

Directions:

- In a blender, combine all the ingredients.
- Until smooth, puree. When needed, taste-test the sweetener.

Nutritional values per serving:
Total Calories: 435kcal, **Fat:** 41g, **Carbohydrates:** 10g, **Protein:** 9g

7. Avocado Berry Smoothie

Ready in: 5 mins.
Serves: 2
Difficulty: easy
Ingredients:

- 1 ⅓ cup of water
- 1 avocado (ripe), peeled & pit removed
- 1-2 tbsp. of lemon juice, about 1 medium lemon
- ½ cup of frozen raspberries (unsweetened) or any other frozen berries (low carb)
- 2 tbsp. of sweetener (low carb), about ⅛ tsp. of liquid stevia extract, as per taste

Directions:

- Blender with all components added.
- Once smooth, blend.
- Pour into two large glasses, then sip via a straw to enjoy!

Nutritional values per serving:
Total Calories: 178kcal, **Fat:** 15g, **Carbohydrates:** 13g, **Protein:** 2g

8. Matcha Green Tea Iced Latte

Ready in: 5 mins.
Serves: 1
Difficulty: easy
Ingredients:

- 1 tsp. of matcha powder 2g
- 1 cup of vanilla almond milk (unsweetened) or coconut milk
- 5 stevia drops (vanilla)

Directions:

- Blend together all the ingredients.
- Mix until all of the matcha powder has dissolved.
- Enjoy after pouring over the ice.

Nutritional values per serving:
Total Calories: 36kcal, **Fat:** 2g, **Carbohydrates:** 1g, **Protein:** 1g

9. Strawberry Coconut Milk Smoothie

Ready in: 5 mins.
Serves: 2
Difficulty: easy
Ingredients:

- 1 cup of unsweetened coconut milk
- 1 cup of strawberries, frozen
- 2 packets of stevia, optional
- 2 tbsp. of smooth almond butter

Directions:

- Blender with all components added.
- Once smooth, blend.
- Pour into a glass, then sip.

Nutritional values per serving:
Total Calories: 397kcal, **Fat:** 37g, **Carbohydrates:** 15g, **Protein:** 6g

10. Green Avocado Mint Smoothie

Ready in: 5 mins.
Serves: 1
Difficulty: easy
Ingredients:

- ¾ cup of coconut milk, full fat
- ½ avocado (about 3 to 4 ounces)
- ½ cup of almond milk
- 5-6 mint leaves (large)
- Sugar substitute (low carb) to taste
- 3 cilantro sprigs
- ¼ tsp. of vanilla
- Some lime juice
- 1 - 1 ½ cups of crushed ice

Directions:

- Blend the items in the blender, except the ice.
- Until fully pureed, blend at low speed.
- Blend in the crushed ice afterward. Adjust sweetness & tartness with a taste. Serve.

Nutritional values per serving:
Total Calories: 223kcal, **Fat:** 23g, **Carbohydrates:** 5g, **Protein:** 1g

CHAPTER 8:
Keto Diet - Dressings, Dips & Sauces Recipes
Dressing & Dips:

1. Ranch Dressing

Ready in: 5 mins.
Serves: 2
Difficulty: easy
Ingredients:

- 1 egg
- 1 cup of avocado oil
- Juice from one lemon, about 2 tbsp.
- 1 tbsp. of dried parsley
- 2 tsp. of Dijon mustard
- 1 tbsp. of dried chives
- 1/2 tsp. of kosher salt
- 1 tsp. of dried dill
- 1/2 tsp. of garlic powder
- 1/4 tsp. of milk
- 1/2 tsp. of onion powder

Directions:

- Add the avocado oil, lemon juice, egg, Dijon mustard, and all the dry spices to a pint-sized Mason jar with a wide opening.
- By pushing the immersion blender all the way into the bottom & enclosing the egg yolk below it, you may add it.
- Use the immersion blender at the bottom for a complete 30 seconds while setting it to high speed. Next, as the egg & oil emulsify, gently bring it to a boil. In essence, you're manufacturing ranch mayonnaise.
- Include 1/4 cup dairy-free milk. Add the blender back in or stir it with a spoon to combine.
- It is best to chill the food for an hour before serving it, allowing the ranch to fully mellow the tastes of the herbs. The longer it's refrigerated, the better it becomes!
- It will last one week in an airtight container.

Nutritional values per serving:
Total Calories: 147kcal, **Fat:** 14g, **Carbohydrates:** 0g, **Protein:** 0g

2. Caesar Salad Dressing

Ready in: 5 mins.
Serves: 2
Difficulty: easy
Ingredients:

- 1 egg (large)
- 1 cup of avocado oil
- zest from one lemon

- 3 garlic cloves, finely minced or grated
- juice from 1/2 a lemon
- 2 tbsp. of nutritional yeast
- 1 tsp. of Dijon mustard
- 1 tbsp. of anchovy paste
- 2-4 tbsp. of plain almond milk, unsweetened
- salt plus pepper, as per taste

Directions:

- A wide-mouth pint Mason jar should be filled with all ingredients except the milk.
- Put the egg yolk in the bottom of the jar and use your immersion blender to puree the mixture. After the immersion blender has been turned on, leave it at bottom for 15 sec. before lifting it up gradually. It will come together like mayonnaise.
- To thin your dressing to the preferred consistency, add the required quantity of almond milk. If necessary, taste and adjust the seasoning.
- It will remain fresh into the Mason jar for at least a week.

Nutritional values per serving:
Total Calories: 131kcal, **Fat:** 14g, **Carbohydrates:** 0g, **Protein:** 1g

3. Buffalo Chicken Dip

Ready in: 20 mins.
Serves: 12
Difficulty: easy
Ingredients:

- 8 ounces of cream cheese in pieces
- 3 cups of chicken, shredded
- 1 cup of mozzarella cheese, shredded
- 1/2 cup of Ranch salad dressing, creamy
- 1/3 cup of Franks Buffalo Sauce
- 2 tbsp. of green onions, chopped

For Garnish:

- 1/3 cup of blue cheese crumbles
- 2 tbsp. of green onions, chopped (or more to taste)

Directions:

- In a medium saucepan or pot, melt the mozzarella and cream cheese over low heat.
- Add the Buffalo sauce and then the chicken after stirring.
- Stir in the green onions and ranch dressing after adding them. Heat the mixture until it is hot. Put in a small appetizer-sized crock pot or a serving dish that has been warmed up.
- Add blue cheese and onions on top.

Nutritional values per serving:
Total Calories: 203kcal, **Fat:** 14g, **Carbohydrates:** 1g, **Protein:** 13g

4. Pizza Dip Supreme

Ready in: 35 mins.
Serves: 6
Difficulty: easy
Ingredients:

- 8 oz. of softened Cream cheese
- 1 link of Italian sausage
- 2 tbsp. of Mayonnaise
- 1 1/2 cups of Mozzarella cheese, Shredded (divided use)
- 1/2 cup of Parmesan cheese, Grated
- 3/4 tsp. of Italian seasoning
- 1 cup of Arrabiata Sauce

- 1/4 tsp. of crushed Fennel seed
- 3 tbsp. of finely diced Green bell pepper
- 2 tbsp. of chopped Black olives
- 3 tbsp. of minced Onion,

Directions:

- Place the rack in the center of the oven and heat it to 350 degrees.
- Sausages should be taken out of their casings and fried in a pan. Be careful to crush it up into little pieces. Drain and cool on paper towels.
- Mix the cream cheese & mayonnaise together in a medium basin. Stirring the ingredients together, add the Italian spice, fennel seed, & 1/3 of each cheese. The base of a baking dish should be covered.
- The cream cheese should be covered with 1/2 cup arrabbiata sauce. Black olives, green bell pepper, onion, and half of the sausage should be distributed. On top, distribute half of the cheese.
- Add the remaining cheese, the remaining sauce, and the remaining sausage & veggies to the dish.
- Bake for 20 to 30 minutes or until heated and bubbling. Instead, cover using cling film & microwave for around 5 minutes based on your microwave. Serve.

Nutritional values per serving:
Total Calories: 346kcal, **Fat:** 28g, **Carbohydrates:** 6g, **Protein:** 15g

5. Creamy Horseradish Bacon Dip

Ready in: 15 mins.
Serves: 6
Difficulty: easy
Ingredients:

- 1/2 cup of Greek Yogurt or sour cream (2%)
- 1/2 cup of mayonnaise
- 4 slices of bacon
- 1 tbsp. of minced green onions
- 1 tbsp. of prepared horseradish
- 1 tsp. of powdered low-carb sugar
- 1/4 tsp. of dried dill weed
- 1/4 tsp. of Worcestershire sauce
- 1/4 tsp. of granulated garlic
- 1/8 tsp. of salt
- 1/8 tsp. of cayenne pepper

Directions:

- Cook chopped bacon over medium heat until crisp. About 6 minutes are

needed for this. Green onions should be minced while you gather the other ingredients.
- All ingredients should be combined and chilled overnight.

Nutritional values per serving:
Total Calories: 172kcal, **Fat:** 18g, **Carbohydrates:** 1g, **Protein:** 4g

6. Curry Cashew Dip

Ready in: 20 mins.
Serves: 8
Difficulty: easy
Ingredients:

- 3/4 cup of vegan mayonnaise
- 1 cup of raw cashews
- 1/3 cup of coconut milk, full fat
- zest of 1 lemon
- 3 tbsp. of lemon juice
- 1/2 tsp. of curry powder
- 1/8 tsp. of garlic powder
- 1/8 tsp. of cayenne pepper
- 1/8 tsp. of salt (or to taste)
- monk fruit or stevia to taste
- 1/8 tsp. of white pepper

Directions:

- Shake the coconut milk can.
- Blend the cashews & mayonnaise until smooth in a low-speed (ice crusher) blender. To speed up the procedure, drizzle in a little coconut milk at a time. You will need to be patient & move around the ingredients the canister & popping any air bubbles that may establish at the bottom if you don't have a good blender.
- Add the rest of ingredients after that. The mixture will become looser as it warms up from friction. To taste and season as necessary.
- Take advantage of this cashew dip right away, or chill it in the fridge. It thickens up significantly when chilled! The flavor is supposedly improved the next day.

Nutritional values per serving:
Total Calories: 199kcal, **Fat:** 20g, **Carbohydrates:** 4g, **Protein:** 2g

7. Spinach Artichoke Dip

Ready in: 30 mins.
Serves: 8
Difficulty: easy
Ingredients:

- 4 oz. of Spinach
- 2 tsp. of Olive oil
- 4 oz. of Cream cheese
- 2 tbsp. of Sour cream (plus 2 tbsp. mayo)
- 2 tbsp. of Mayonnaise
- 1/4 cup of parmesan cheese, Grated
- 4 cloves of Garlic (minced)
- 1 can of Artichoke hearts in water, drained (14.5 oz.), (chopped & squeezed)
- 2/3 cup of shredded Mozzarella cheese (divided into two parts)
- 1/4 tsp. of Black pepper

Directions:

- Heat the oil in a medium frying pan over a medium flame. Spinach is now added. Stirring periodically, cook the spinach for 2 to 3 minutes or until it is wilted and brilliant green. (Alternatively, microwave the spinach for 2 to 3 minutes to wilt it.)

Set alone for cooling. You may put the bowl in a bigger bowl filled with ice to hasten the chilling process (optional).

- Heat the oven up to 350 degrees Fahrenheit while the spinach cools (177 degrees C).
- In the meanwhile, warm the cream cheese into the microwave or over low heat in a medium pan on the stove. Add the sour cream, mayonnaise, grated parmesan cheese, minced garlic, chopped artichoke hearts, black pepper, & half of the mozzarella after it has melted enough to mix. To blend, stir.
- Squeeze the spinach several times when it has cooled enough to handle, being careful to extract as much water as you can. To the artichoke mixture, add the spinach.
- Transfer your dip to a large ramekin or small porcelain appetizer plate. Smooth the top using a spatula. Top with the remaining mozzarella shavings.
- Bake for 20 to 30 minutes or until bubbling and heated. Serve hot.

Nutritional values per serving:
Total Calories: 133kcal, **Fat:** 11g, **Carbohydrates:** 2g, **Protein:** 4g

8. Tzatziki Dip

Ready in: 5 mins.
Serves: 6
Difficulty: easy
Ingredients:

- 1 ⅕ cups of Greek yogurt
- 1 cucumber (English), seeded & finely diced
- 4 tbsp. of olive oil
- 2 tbsp. of dill (fresh), chopped
- 1 tbsp. of lemon juice
- 2 tbsp. of minced garlic
- 1 tsp. of pepper
- 1 tsp. of sea salt

Directions:

- Slice, seed, and finely cut the cucumber.
- Mix all items together well.
- For optimum taste, refrigerate the dip overnight.

Nutritional values per serving:
Total Calories: 121kcal, **Fat:** 10g, **Carbohydrates:** 3g, **Protein:** 4g

9. Hot Baked Onion Dip

Ready in: 45 mins.
Serves: 12
Difficulty: easy
Ingredients:

- 1 tbsp. of butter
- 1 yellow onion
- 8 ounces of cream cheese (normal temp)
- 2 cups of cheese, shredded (any)
- 1/2 cup of mayo
- 1 tsp. of garlic powder
- Garnish with chives or parsley
- 1 tbsp. of Tabasco sauce

Optional:

- 1/4 tsp. of flakes of red pepper

Directions:

- Sauté your onions in 1 tbsp. Butter in a small frying pan.
- The sautéed onions, cream cheese, mayonnaise, tabasco sauce, shredded cheese, and red pepper flakes, if

used, should all be combined in a medium bowl.
- The components should be well mixed.
- Bake for 25 to 30 minutes, or until golden brown, at 350 degrees.
- Serve with pork rinds, celery, green, red, or slices of orange bell pepper, keto chips, or all of the above!

Nutritional values per serving:
Total Calories: 201kcal, **Fat:** 18g, **Carbohydrates:** 3g, **Protein:** 6g

10. Cheese Sausage Dip

Ready in: 25 mins.
Serves: 16
Difficulty: easy
Ingredients:

- 1 cup of diced tomatoes
- 12 ounces of bulk Italian sausage
- 2 jalapeños (medium), finely minced
- 8 ounces of cheddar cheese, shredded
- 8 ounces of cream cheese in small pieces

Directions:

- Sauté the sausage for 8 to 10 minutes, or until it is well cooked, in a 10-inch skillet set over medium heat. If the fat in the sausage is very thick, spoon some of it out.
- Bring to a simmer after adding the tomatoes and jalapenos.
- Get rid of the heat. Stirring helps the cheese melt, so add both slices of cheese, cover the pan, and let it aside for approximately 5 minutes.
- Spread evenly into the pan after removing the lid and stirring well. Serve warm with low-carb crackers and vegetables.

Nutritional values per serving:
Total Calories: 183kcal, **Fat:** 13g, **Carbohydrates:** 2g, **Protein:** 8g

Sauces

1. Mixed Nut Butter Sauce

Ready in: 25 mins.
Serves: 2
Difficulty: easy
Ingredients:

- 1 cup of raw pecans
- 2 cups of raw almonds
- 1 tsp. of kosher salt
- 1/2 cup of raw cashews

Directions:

- On a baking sheet with a rim, arrange all raw nuts evenly. Roast for 15 to 20 minutes at 350°F or until golden brown.
- Add the heated nuts directly from the oven into your food processor, together with 1 tsp. Kosher salt. Smooth and creamy results from processing for 10 minutes, scraping the bowl down occasionally.
- For at least four weeks, keep it in a pint glass jar in the refrigerator.

Nutritional values per serving:
Total Calories: 175kcal, **Fat:** 15g, **Carbohydrates:** 6g, **Protein:** 5g

2. Pesto Aioli Sauce

Ready in: 10 mins.
Serves: 2
Difficulty: easy
Ingredients:

- 1/4 cup of homemade pesto
- 1 batch of homemade mayo, almost 1 to 3/4 cups

Directions:

- Mayo and pesto should be combined in a Mason jar. To blend, stir.
- Serve right away or keep chilled for up to 8-10 days.

Nutritional values per serving:
Total Calories: 169kcal, **Fat:** 18g, **Carbohydrates:** 0g, **Protein:** 0g

3. Tartar Sauce

Ready in: 5 mins.
Serves: 1
Difficulty: easy
Ingredients:

- 4 tbsp. of pickles, finely chopped
- 1 cup of mayonnaise
- 1 tbsp. of pickle juice

Directions:

- Combine the mayo, diced pickles, and pickle juice in a small dish or container. To blend, stir.
- Serve the seafood at room temperature or chilled.
- Will stay chilled for at least a week in an airtight container.

Nutritional values per serving:
Total Calories: 188kcal, **Fat:** 20g, **Carbohydrates:** 0g, **Protein:** 0g

4. Marinara Sheet Pan Sauce

Ready in: 2 hrs. 5 mins.
Serves: 6
Difficulty: medium
Ingredients:

- 1 chopped yellow onion
- 8 cups of tomatoes
- 6 garlic cloves, whole
- 2 tsp. of kosher salt
- 1/3 cup of olive oil
- 1/2 cup of packed fresh basil

Directions:

- Set the oven to 350°F. Use parchment paper to line a baking sheet with a rim.
- On the baking sheet, spread the tomatoes, onion, and garlic out. Add salt and a drizzle of olive oil.
- For two hours, cook slowly in the oven. After removing, let the food cool to normal temperature.
- The tomato mixture should be added to your high-speed blender after you remove the parchment paper. Fresh basil should be added.
- Mix at a medium or low speed until the required consistency is achieved. If extra salt is required, taste the food beforehand.
- Fill pint-sized Mason jars with a wide mouth with the marinara sauce. There will be plenty for 3 mason jars since this recipe yields 6 cups. Make sure that you don't exceed the "freeze" line if frozen!
- It will last at least a week in the refrigerator, at least six months in the freezer, or a year in the deep freezer.

Nutritional values per serving:
Total Calories: 79kcal, **Fat:** 6g, **Carbohydrates:** 5g, **Protein:** 1g

5. Hollandaise Sauce

Ready in: 5 mins.
Serves: 1
Difficulty: easy

Ingredients:

- 1/3 cup of ghee, melted
- 4 egg yolks (large)
- 2 tbsp. of water
- 1/2 tsp. of kosher salt
- 1 tbsp. of lemon juice

Directions:

- In a pint-sized Mason jar with a wide opening, combine the salt and egg yolks. The egg yolks should be blended for 30 seconds using an immersion blender.
- Combine the water, melted ghee, and lemon juice into a measuring cup along with a pour spout. To blend, stir.
- Pour the melted ghee mixture gradually into the Mason jar while your immersion blender is still running. Every 5 seconds, raise your immersion blender & push it back down to aid in emulsifying the liquid. Add the remaining melted ghee mixture after a while.
- Add additional as required after tasting for salt & lemon juice.
- Top poached eggs, veggies, salmon, chicken, or fish with the heated mixture.
- It will last a week when kept chilled into a mason jar.
- Microwave one cup of water in a measuring cup (2 cups) for 3 minutes to rewarm from the refrigeration. To make a water bath, submerge the Glass jar into warm water. As soon as the mixture is heated, shake the jar once every few minutes.

Nutritional values per serving:
Total Calories: 96kcal, **Fat:** 9g, **Carbohydrates:** 0g, **Protein:** 1g

6. Cashew Cream

Ready in: 5 mins.
Serves: 1
Difficulty: easy
Ingredients:

- 1/2 cup of water
- 1 cup of cashews (raw), dipped overnight in 1 and a half cups of water

Directions:

- The cashews should be drained and washed.
- To your high-speed blender, add soaked cashews & a new 1/2 cup of water. Blend for two minutes at high speed, scraping the sides down halfway through.
- Will keep it in the fridge for one week.
- Use cream in sauces & other dishes at a 1:1 ratio.

Nutritional values per serving:
Total Calories: 79kcal, **Fat:** 6g, **Carbohydrates:** 4g, **Protein:** 2g

7. Orange Parsley Sauce

Ready in: 5 mins.
Serves: 2
Difficulty: easy
Ingredients:

- 1/2 cup of olive oil
- 1 cup of parsley leaves (packed), some stems ok
- 1/2 cup of unsalted roasted pecans

- juice from one orange, almost about 1/4 cup
- zest from one orange
- 1/2 tsp. of salt
- 2 garlic cloves

Directions:

- In a food processor, combine all the ingredients and pulse till it resembles pesto. If necessary, taste and adjust the seasoning.
- Serve with seafood, meat, or veggies! Yummy on everything!
- It will last two weeks in the airtight container or six months in the freezer.

Nutritional values per serving:
Total Calories: 58kcal, **Fat:** 5g, **Carbohydrates:** 2g, **Protein:** 1g

8. Chimichurri Sauce

Ready in: 5 mins.
Serves: 2
Difficulty: easy
Ingredients:

- 1 bunch of cilantro leaves
- 1 bunch of parsley leaves
- 3/4 cup of olive oil
- 3 garlic cloves
- 1/4 cup of red wine vinegar
- 1 tsp. of flakes of red pepper, optional
- 1/2 tsp. of pepper
- 1/2 tsp. of salt

Directions:

- Use a food processor to blend all the ingredients together. Once mixed, pulse for approximately 30-45 seconds.
- Pour over cooked meat, fish, and veggies.
- In a pint Mason jar or airtight container, leftovers may be frozen for up to six months or kept in the fridge for 14 days.

Nutritional values per serving:
Total Calories: 65kcal, **Fat:** 5g, **Carbohydrates:** 4g, **Protein:** 1g

9. Cheese Sauce

Ready in: 10 mins.
Serves: 10
Difficulty: easy
Ingredients:

- 1 cup of Butter
- 8 ounces of Cream Cheese
- 2 cups of mozzarella cheese
- 1 cup of Heavy Cream

Directions:

- The cream cheese, butter, and heavy cream should be combined in a skillet and heated slowly.
- Stirring should continue until all ingredients are mixed, and the cream cheese gets melted.
- After the mozzarella cheese has been added, keep whisking until it has melted and been well mixed.
- Use the sauce right away or put it in the refrigerator. Reheat while continually whisking over low heat.

Nutritional values per serving:
Total Calories: 389kcal, **Fat:** 39g, **Carbohydrates:** 2g, **Protein:** 6g

10. Enchilada Sauce

Ready in: 15 mins.
Serves: 8
Difficulty: easy
Ingredients:

- 3 tsp. of Cumin ground
- 1/3 cup of Salted Butter
- 2 tsp. of Dried Oregano
- 2 tsp. of Onion Powder
- 2 tsp. of Coriander ground
- 1/4 tsp. of Cayenne Pepper ground
- 12 ounces of Tomato Puree
- 1 1/2 tbsp. of Erythritol
- 1/2 tsp. of ground pepper
- 1/2 tsp. of Salt

Directions:

- Put a pot with the butter over medium heat.
- Melt the butter.
- Including the tomato puree, add all the ingredients and cook for 3 mins or till aromatic.
- Components of keto enchilada sauce.
- Stir thoroughly after adding the tomato puree.
- For the spices to fully meld, simmer the sauce for 5 minutes. If you like a thinner sauce, add a little water, and taste-test the spice.
- Use right immediately or let to cool for 30-35 minutes before putting it in a heatproof jar & keeping for up to 1-2 weeks in the refrigerator.

Nutritional values per serving:
Total Calories: 90kcal, **Fat:** 8g, **Carbohydrates:** 4g, **Protein:** 1g

28-Day Meal Plan

Following is the meal plan for 28 days having recipes from previous chapters in the order number as mentioned in their respective chapter.

Week 1:

Day 1:

Breakfast:

1. Green Eggs (pg. 25)

30. Peanut Butter Chocolate Smoothie (pg. 41)

Lunch:

1. Portobello Mushroom Burger (pg. 42)

Snack:

3. Zucchini Chips (pg. 88)

Dinner:

1. Lasagna (pg. 64)

Day 2:

Breakfast:

3. Pancakes (pg. 26)

8. Olive & Basil Eggs (pg. 28)

Lunch:

5. No Bean Chili (pg. 45)

6. Chicken Avocado Salad (pg. 46)

Snack:

10. Buffalo Chicken Delicious Celery Sticks (pg. 93)

7. Cheesy Garlic Bread (pg. 91)

Dinner:

3. Creamy Tuscan Salmon (pg. 73)

Day 3:

Breakfast:

7. Crustless Quiche (pg. 28)

Lunch:

2. Zucchini Pizza (pg. 43)

16. Broccoli Stir-Fry with Garlic Sauce (pg. 52)

Snack:

5. Taco Cups (pg. 89)

1. Chicken Fajita Soup (pg. 109)

Dinner:

2. Beef Tips with Gravy (pg. 64)

4. Potato Cauliflower Salad (pg. 124)

Day 4:

Breakfast:

4. Masala Frittata & Avocado Salsa (pg. 26)

Lunch:

6. Lemon Pesto Zoodles (pg. 46)

9. Sunflower Seed Cheese Courgetti (pg. 47)

Snack:

1. Jalapeno Poppers (pg. 95)

Dinner:

3. Meatloaf (pg. 65)

4. Enchilada Stuffed Delicious Zucchini Boats (pg. 66)

Day 5:

Breakfast:

5. Courgette Frittatas (pg. 27)

Lunch:

10. Street Tacos (pg. 48)

Snack:

2. Chicken Nuggets (pg. 95)

Dinner:

5. Ground Beef Pizza Casserole (pg. 66)

Day 6:

Breakfast:

6. Mushroom, Ham & Spinach Frittata (pg. 27)

Lunch:

11. Creamy Brussels Sprout Spaghetti (pg. 48)

Snack:

3. Cheese Ball with Bacon, Cream Cheese & Green Onion (pg. 96)

Dinner:

6. Bacon Cheeseburger Casserole (pg. 67)

Day 7:

Breakfast:

8. Olive & Basil Eggs (pg. 28)

Lunch:

13. Shepherd's Pie (pg. 50)

Snack:

4. Buffalo Chicken Wings (pg. 97)

Dinner:

7. Instant Pot Meatballs (pg. 68)

Week 2:

Day 1:

Breakfast:

10. Avocado & Bacon Frittata (pg. 29)

Lunch:

14. Peanut Butter Tofu & Sriracha (pg. 51)

Snack:

5. Nachos with Spicy Chicken (pg. 97)

Dinner:

8. Lamb Chops with Chutney (pg. 68)

Day 2:

Breakfast:

11. Kale & Mushroom brunch (pg. 30)

Lunch:

16. Broccoli Stir-Fry with Garlic Sauce (pg. 52)

2. Tomato Basil & Mozzarella Galette (pg. 56)

Snack:

6. Almond Flour Crackers (pg. 98)

Dinner:

9. Lamb Shish Kabobs & Grilled Vegetables (pg. 69)

Day 3:

Breakfast:

12. Scrambled Eggs with Spinach, Basil & Tomatoes (pg. 30)

Lunch:

3. Tuscan Creamy Garlic Chicken (pg. 57)

Snack:

7. Cauliflower Breadsticks (pg. 98)

Dinner:

10. Baked Pork Chops with Onion Gravy (pg. 70)

Day 4:

Breakfast:

13. Herby Omelette (pg. 31)

Lunch:

4. Spinach & Goat Cheese Stuffed Chicken Breast with Mushrooms & Caramelized Onions (pg. 58)

Snack:

8. Baked Zucchini Fries (pg. 99)

Dinner:

1. Garlic Butter Lemon Shrimp & Zucchini Noodles (pg. 71)

Day 5:

Breakfast:

14. Pancetta Avocado Soldiers With Soft-Boiled Eggs (pg. 31)

Lunch:

5. Chicken Enchilada Bowl (pg. 59)

Snack:

9. Mozzarella Sticks (pg. 100)

Dinner:

2. Baked Asparagus Salmon in Foil (pg. 72)

Day 6:

Breakfast:

15. Spinach and Sprout Baked Eggs (pg. 32)

Lunch:

8. Chicken Caprese (pg. 61)

Snack:

10. Onion Rings (pg. 10)

Dinner:

3. Creamy Tuscan Salmon (pg. 73)

Day 7:

Breakfast:

16. Bun-less Egg, Bacon & Cheese (pg. 32)

Lunch:

9. Chicken Thighs (pg. 62)

8. Stuffed Avocado Salad (pg. 126)

Snack:

3. Italian Stuffed Baked Artichokes with Sausage (pg. 103)

Dinner:

4. Bacon Salmon (pg. 73)

Week 3:

Day 1:

Breakfast:

17. Cinnamon Rolls (pg. 33)

Lunch:

19. Fried Mac and Cheese (pg. 55)

10. Buffalo Chicken Salad (pg. 127)

Snack:

2. Zuppa Toscana Soup (pg. 110)

Dinner:

5. Salmon Cakes (pg. 75)

Day 2:

Breakfast:

18. Egg, Ham & Cheese Roll-Ups (pg. 33)

Lunch:

18. Sesame Tofu & Eggplant (pg. 54)

Snack:

7. Cabbage Beef Soup (pg. 113)

Dinner:

6. Baked Cod (pg. 75)

Day 3:

Breakfast:

19. Pumpkin Pie (pg. 34)

Lunch:

1. Cauliflower Mac and Cheese (pg. 56)

Snack:

10. Tomato Soup (pg. 115)

Dinner:

7. Pad Thai & Shirataki Noodles (pg. 76)

Day 4:

Breakfast:

20. Almond Flour Crepes (pg. 35)

Lunch:

17. Three Cheese Stuffed Peppers Quiche (pg. 53)

Snack:

3. Broccoli Bacon Salad (pg. 124)

Dinner:

8. Garlic Butter Baked Lobster Tails (pg. 77)

Day 5:

Breakfast:

22. Almond Flour Waffles (pg. 36)

Lunch:

11. Creamy Brussels Sprout Spaghetti (pg. 48)

Snack:

6. Chicken Avocado Salad (pg. 125)

Dinner:

9. Tuna Casserole (pg. 77)

Day 6:

Breakfast:

23. Granola Cereal (pg. 36)

Lunch:

4. Almond Butter Lettuce Wraps (pg. 44)

20. Red Coconut Curry (pg. 55)

Snack:

3. Cheese Ball with Bacon, Cream Cheese & Green Onion (pg. 96)

Dinner:

10. Shrimp & Spinach Cream Sauce (pg. 78)

Day 7:

Breakfast:

24. Egg Muffins (pg. 37)

Lunch:

3. Tuscan Creamy Garlic Chicken (pg. 57)

Snack:

5. Nachos with Spicy Chicken (pg. 97)

Dinner:

11. Pan Seared Scallops & Lemon Garlic Sauce (pg. 78)

Week 4:

Day 1:

Breakfast:

25. Cheddar Broccoli Quiche (pg. 38)

Lunch:

6. White Chicken Chili (pg. 59)

Snack:

7. Cauliflower Breadsticks (pg. 98)

Dinner:

12. Basil Garlic Butter Steamed Clams (pg. 80)

13. Bacon Crab Stuffed Mushrooms (pg. 80)

Day 2:

Breakfast:

26. Breakfast Yogurt (pg. 39)

15. Spinach and Sprout Baked Eggs (pg. 32)

Lunch:

8. Chicken Caprese (pg. 61)

Snack:

1. Jalapeno Poppers (pg. 95)

Dinner:

14. Mahi Mahi with Salsa & Feta (pg. 81)

Day 3:

Breakfast:

29. Protein Shake (pg. 40)

27. Oatmeal (pg. 39)

Lunch:

10. White Wine Delicious Coq au Vin (pg. 63)

Snack:

10. Buffalo Chicken Delicious Celery Sticks (pg. 93)

Dinner:

15. Fish Pie (pg. 81)

Day 4:

Breakfast:

20. Almond Flour Crepes (pg. 35)

28. Coffee (pg. 40)

Lunch:

7. Lemon Chicken Skewers & Tzatziki Sauce (pg. 60)

Snack:

7. Cheesy Garlic Bread (pg. 91)

Dinner:

16. Coconut Spinach Fish Curry (pg. 83)

Day 5:

Breakfast:

24. Egg Muffins (pg. 37)

Lunch:

10. Street Tacos (pg. 48)

14. Peanut Butter Tofu & Sriracha (pg. 51)

Snack:

4. Cucumber Smoked Salmon Bites (pg. 89)

Dinner:

19. Shrimp Lettuce Wraps (pg. 84)

Day 6:

Breakfast:

14. Pancetta Avocado Soldiers With Soft-Boiled Eggs (pg. 31)

Lunch:

18. Sesame Tofu & Eggplant (pg. 54)

Snack:

4. Buffalo Chicken Wings (pg. 97)

Dinner:

6. Bacon Cheeseburger Casserole (pg. 67)

Day 7:

Breakfast:

13. Herby Omelette (pg. 31)

Lunch:

20. Red Coconut Curry (pg. 55)

Snack:

8. Baked Zucchini Fries (pg. 99)

Dinner:

9. Lamb Shish Kabobs & Grilled Vegetables (pg. 69)

CONCLUSION

The ketogenic diet is a way of eating that places emphasis on meals that include significant quantities of protein, healthy fats, and low carbs. Consuming more energy from fat than from carbohydrates is the objective. The diet involves decreasing the body's supply of sugar. It will therefore start to digest fat for energy. As a consequence, the body begins to produce molecules known as ketones, which it utilizes as fuel. Weight loss may result from the body burning fat. Generally speaking, foods like high-fat meats, oils, fish, nuts, high-fat dairy products like cheese, & low-carb vegetables like leafy greens are permitted. Consequently, reducing carb consumption necessitates staying away from typical baked goods like bread, rice, and pasta. Nevertheless, avoiding legumes, the majority of fruits, root vegetables, & starchy vegetables such as potatoes is necessary to get such low carbohydrate levels.

The keto diet may aid individuals in consuming fewer calories overall since proteins and fats have more satiating power than carbohydrates do. There is a lot of research being done on the ketogenic diet and various medical disorders, such as epilepsy, where it may reduce seizure frequency. Most people may comfortably follow a keto when it is properly organized and takes into consideration all nutrition-related aspects. Although consuming certain vitamins and minerals may be more difficult, meal planning or taking supplements may be helpful.

INDEX

2

3

4

5

6

7

8

Made in the USA
Monee, IL
22 April 2023

d4bb3a5a-59bb-4771-bdd2-b73f733b6a72R01